Wilderstein
and the Suckleys

Wilderstein and the Suckleys

A Hudson River Legacy

BY CYNTHIA OWEN PHILIP

INTRODUCTION BY GEOFFREY C. WARD

Wilderstein Preservation

RHINEBECK, NEW YORK

2001

Published by Wilderstein Preservation,
P. O. Box 383, Rhinebeck, New York 12572

Preservation and conservation of the archive and photograph collections, and preparation and publication of this book have been assisted by grants from
The Samuel H. Kress Foundation,
The New York State Conservation/Preservation Program, and
Furthermore, the publication program of the J. M. Kaplan Fund.

Library of Congress Catalogue Number: 2001130401
ISBN 0-9706846-0-6

Photograph opposite title page:
Platinotype by Rockwood Studios, New York, 1895.
Margaret Lynch Suckley, "Daisy," (1891-1991), aged 4.

Front cover photograph: Jay Olstad
Back cover photograph: Anne Liljedahl Schock
Color section photographs:
Steve Gross and Susan Daley #2, 4, 5, 8
John E. Kane and Wendy Carlson #1, 3, 6, 7

Typeset in Bembo and produced by Bound to Last,
a division of McPherson & Company, Kingston, New York.
Design by Bruce R. McPherson.
Printed in the United States of America.

INTRODUCTION

FOR THOSE NOT FORTUNATE enough to have visited Wilderstein when Daisy Suckley was in residence and in charge, Cynthia Owen Philip has performed an invaluable service. Through a rare combination of scrupulous research and vivid writing, she has made that most lived-in of all the great Hudson River houses live again; has peopled its crowded rooms with all the members of the complicated Suckley clan who called them home for more than a century.

The Suckleys turn out to have been memorable not for what they accomplished in the wider world, perhaps, but for who they were as human beings, for what they meant to one another, and for the extraordinary world they created for themselves high above their beloved river. This is a fine book about a splendid house.

GEOFFREY C. WARD

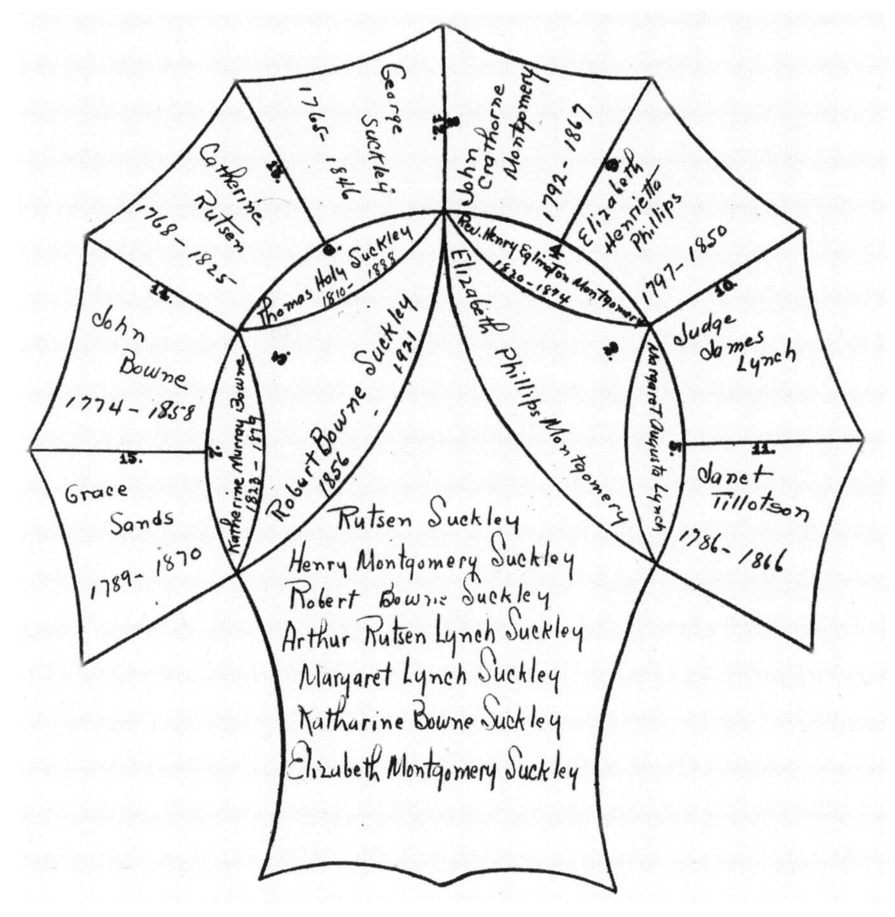

The Suckley lineage. Four generations of an eight generation genealogical fan chart in Margaret Lynch ("Daisy") Suckley's hand.

Wilderstein the First

1856

1888

SET SO HIGH ON A BLUFF ABOVE THE Hudson River that on a clear day the rift in the headlands thirty miles to the south can be seen from its exuberant five-story tower, Wilderstein stands a resplendent example of America's Queen Anne style of architecture. Its intricately framed verandahs, decorated gables and rich period interiors capture the playful creativity of the gilded age. The walks and gardens, laid out by the premier landscape architect, Calvert Vaux, together with the gazebos, carriage house, ice house, potting shed, and Gate Lodge, envelop Wilderstein in a magical world of its own.

Although the immediate impression is of fancy let loose—Wilderstein seems more like a fairy tale stage set than a residence—it was created for a rapidly growing family and constantly visiting relatives to live in and enjoy. The necessary array of servants served their needs. Multiple cats, dogs, cows, goats, and horses made themselves at home there, too. All put their mark on Wilderstein. And, to an extraordinary degree, Wilderstein put its mark on them. Still, with the vital exception of the site, the house and grounds reflect the vision of one man, Robert Bowne Suckley.

Robert was born at Wilderstein in 1856 and grew up there. At that time the house was a modest two-storied Italianate villa, sober even for its day. Built four years earlier by his father, Thomas Holy Suckley, as a home for his bride, Catharine Murray Bowne, it possessed little of the sublime ornamentation treasured by Romantic era architects. In plan it was almost a square. The low Tuscan roof rested on brackets of simple design. The roofs of the entrance porch and the verandah that wrapped around the south and west sides were supported by square paneled pillars. There was no tower to provide the expected varied profile. Although undoubtedly comfortable, the effect was of reticent solidity.

When Thomas Holy Suckley decided to build this villa, he was forty-two years old, well-educated, well-traveled, and experienced enough in the pleasures and pressures of New York City living to know that he preferred the leisurely life of a country gentleman. He had the wealth to afford it. He was heir, with his older brother Rutsen and sister Mary, to a large fortune, accumulated by his father George who, in 1784, had emigrated from Sheffield, England to the United States, as the agent for a manufacturer of hardware—adzes, teapots, surgical instruments, and even toupee curling irons. George prospered in trade and shipping along the United States coast, the West Indies, and South America. It was he who put the first commercial steamboat on Colombia's Lake Maracaibo. By 1846, when he died, George had parlayed these enterprises into vast holdings of real estate concentrated in New York City, Jersey City, Newark, and Hoboken. In addition, his wife, Catherine Rutsen, whose father was a direct descendant of the powerful Beekman and Livingston clans, brought significant northern Dutchess County land into the family.

This handsome inheritance was expertly managed by Thomas's older brother Rutsen who gave him an allowance of three thousand dollars a year with extra stipends when special circumstances arose. (At this time an exceptionally accomplished artisan might earn three dollars a day.) Since both

Bold projections were the hallmark of the ideal Italianate villa. Rendering by John Warren Ritch for his pattern book, *The American Architect, Part I*. N.Y., 1847.

Rutsen and Mary had remained single, Thomas could anticipate a substantial fortune in his own name. Moreover, like his mother Catherine Rutsen, his wife, Catharine Murray Bowne, came from a family possessing much property in the Rhinebeck area.

Unfortunately, none of the land owned by the Suckleys or the Bownes overlooked the Hudson River, the top prerequisite for both Thomas and Catharine. They would have to buy. That was not easily accomplished, for not only was most such land still in the hands of Livingston descendants, but the construction of the Hudson River Railroad was placing what little was available in high demand. Fortunately, after considering a property in Hyde Park and an eighteenth-century Kip house in the Rhinebeck hamlet of Rhinecliff, Thomas was offered an ideal 32 1/4 acres, located just two miles south of the Rhinecliff steamboat and ferry landing and the railroad stop.

Top: George Suckley (1765-1846) English immigrant, devout Methodist and founder of the family fortune. Miniature on ivory, c. 1796. *Bottom:* Catherine Rutsen Suckley (1768-1825) Beekman/Livingston descendant, mother of seven. Engraving by J. C. Buttre.

The property belonged to Mary Rutherford Garrettson, the only daughter of the Reverend Freeborn Garrettson, a prominent American Methodist and Catherine Livingston Garrettson, another Beekman-Livingston decendant. "Cousin Mary" was only distantly related to the Suckleys, but the families had long been intimate, their initial bond being their strong Methodist faith. Because she was the last of her line—she was an only child and a spinster—Mary was happy to sell her north field to a trusted friend.

The site was one of the most beautiful on the east bank of the Hudson River. It possessed all the "rich and varied charms" extolled by the great Romantic landscape architect Andrew Jackson Downing, whom Thomas so much admired. That the land was largely ill-suited for farming, because of the steep ravine-cut bluff, was an advantage. It had been used most recently to graze sheep and, with the exception of some hedgerow cedars, there were few trees to obstruct the long view down the stately Hudson, so wide at that point that it resembled a lake. Across the river, to the northwest, rose the spires of the town of Kingston and the multilayered Catskill Mountains. Bordering on the north and east was the well-kept estate called

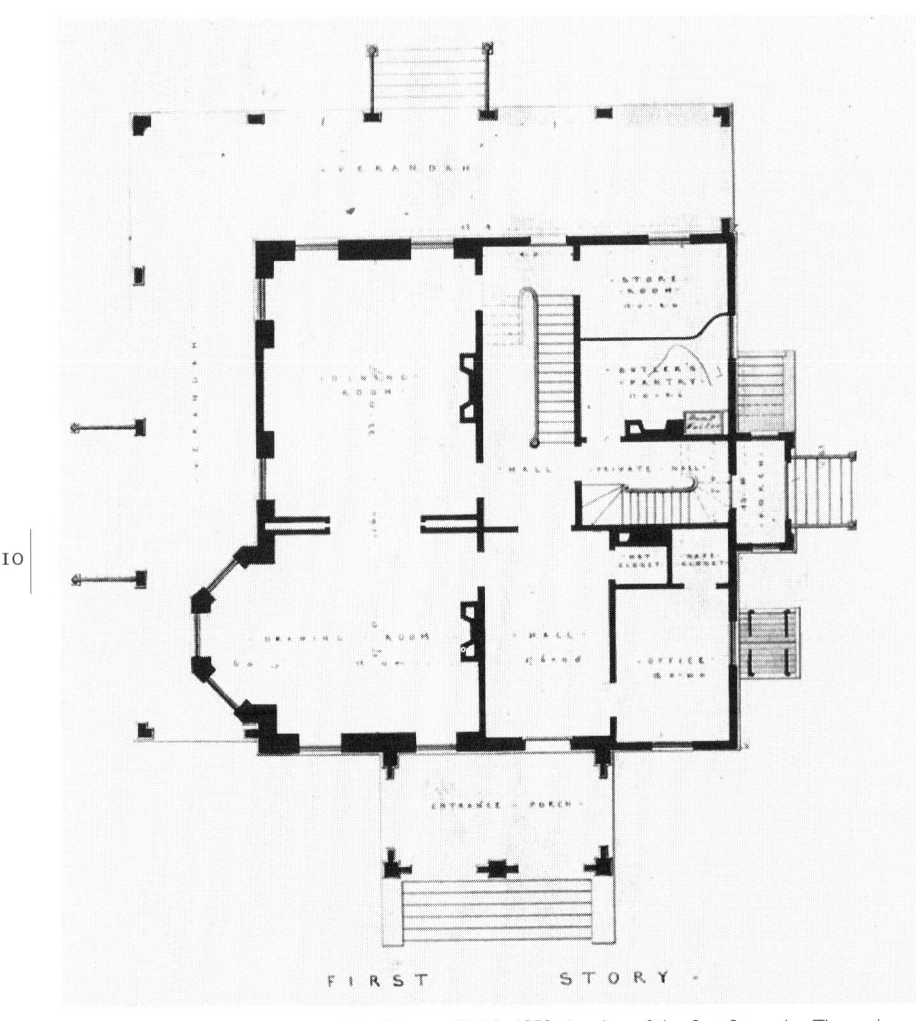

John Warren Ritch's 1852 drawing of the first floor plan. The main entrance was through double doors on the right of the porch.

Ellerslie, once Livingston property, but then owned by New York City merchant William Kelly. On August 14, 1852, Thomas signed an agreement to pay just over $150 an acre for the property. It was a reasonable price for the parcel, the practical Rutsen told him, characteristically adding: "if you have the quantity indicated, there will be comparatively little new fence to be made and kept up afterwards."

Thomas immediately engaged an architect, the young John Warren Ritch, who had made substantial renovations for Rutsen on a family-owned property in New York City. That Thomas chose to have an architect at all was in itself a measure of his expectations. Good house plans, complete with carpenters' and masons' specifications, were readily available. Moreover, builders were not above pirating the designs of houses they had worked on. There is every indication, for instance, that the Bownes' Hill Top Farm in the eastern section of Rhinebeck was copied from Alexander Jackson Davis's Delamater House in the village. That Thomas chose a New York City architect, when Davis's and Downing's partner Calvert Vaux was active in the area, suggests that he relied on Rutsen's advice. (Downing had died that July in a tragic steamboat explosion.) Rutsen, whose permanent residence was the family house at 103 St. Mark's Place in New York City, had misgivings about rural builders' capability. Ritch was a known entity. Among the fine architecture and landscape materials preserved in the Wilderstein archives are leaves from Ritch's pattern book, *The American Architect*, in which, imitating Downing and Vaux, he presented styles ranging from Gothic and Italianate to Elizabethan and rustic.

Thomas chose the Italianate. Ritch describes it as "singularly appropriate for Country residences and ornate villas besides affording ample range to combine the useful and the beautiful... The Turret or Square Tower is peculiar to Buildings of this style; and no feature can be introduced with more advantage for architectural variety." Downing's description of the Italianate was even more to the point. It is, he said, "remarkable for expressing the elegant culture and variety of refinement of the retired citizen or man of the world...not wholly the spirit of country life nor of town life, but a mingling of both."

It was, however, a bare-bones version of the Italianate that Thomas, or perhaps the frugal Rutsen, specified. It had no projecting tower nor little balconies nor elaborately bracketed roof supports, nor setbacks to heighten the effect of light and shade. Yet, its spareness could not have been a matter of economy, for the house would cost $8,500, more than twice Ritch's more embellished, though smaller, prototype. Rather, the floor plan reflects the simplicity of Federal houses, with rooms arranged for convenience as well as elegance.

The drawing room, with its eastern exposure and southern polygonal bay, and the dining room with windows on both the south and west would have been flooded with light in all seasons. Each had a fireplace. When the wide sliding doors between them were open, the space was over forty feet long. Upstairs were four bedrooms, two dressing rooms, a linen closet, and a centrally positioned bathroom with a bathtub and water closet. ("Deafening"—strips of wood covered with plaster—was added to the floor beams so that the water flowing through the plumbing would not resound throughout the house.) Two small rooms for servants occupied part of the attic; the rest was designated storage space. The basement kitchen was connected to a butler's pantry near the dining room by a dumb waiter, an old fashioned arrangement that had been out of favor for some time.

The house was built of wood, the outer walls filled with brick. The exterior was flush-laid pine board. Henry Latson of Rhinebeck was the carpenter and D. Whipple the plasterer. The mason was T. Bird, originally brought up from New York City to work on Wyndcliffe, a massive brick mansion on the river to the south. (That villa would become the model for Edith Wharton's *Hudson River Bracketed.)* C. N. O'Hara of Poughkeepsie installed the plumbing. At least fourteen laborers and artisans worked on the project. Their pay ranged from one dollar a day to four dollars and fifty cents for a man and a horse.

On December 23, 1852, Thomas wrote triumphantly in his leather-bound record book: "Commenced digging out the cellar for the new House." Construction progressed throughout the winter on a barn and stable and an icehouse as well as on the dwelling. On February 24, 1853, he confidently declared in a letter to Rutsen, "I rather think the Month of May will not pass, before we are snugly stowed, perhaps in a *dressing room.*" Nevertheless, Catharine, who was expecting their first child toward the end of June, had doubts that the house would be habitable before autumn. She was right. Work stretched on through the summer. Baby Rutsen was born on July 3. The joyous event, Thomas noted in his daybook, was celebrated with biscuit and cake all around. It was not until November that he wrote with jubilant brevity: "Commenced Housekeeping at 'The Cedars.'" At the end of January 1854, he stated with equal pleasure: "Paid Latson & O'Hara in full."

Meanwhile, the work of landscaping proceeded informally. It is almost certain that the soil from the cellar excavation was used to level and extend the south lawn. In April 1854, Thomas recorded having "transplanted evergreens" and "dropped a few Mountain ash seeds." In May he planted a larch, the gift of Mary Garrettson, to supplement the wild locusts and cedars that grew on the rugged bluff. In 1854 he ordered four sugar maples, two balm of Gilead poplars, two weeping willows and two white elms. He also planted a long, rectangular orchard on the east-west slope south of the house. It contained ten varieties of apples, among them Bishop pippins, Rhode Island greenings, Northern Spies, Baldwins, Siberian crabs, and Esopus spitzenbergers; nine varieties of peaches, seven of pears, seven of plums, six of cherries, and two quince and two apricot trees. Although farming would never become more than a gentleman's hobby, his daybooks record such events as the planting of peas, beets, radishes, turnips, corn, potatoes, and other vegetables, the breeding of cows and horses, the collecting of eggs, and the killing of hogs, turkeys, and chickens.

It was probably at this time that the Suckleys decided to change the name of the property from The Cedars to Wilderstein as more in keeping with the vogue for romantic names. Wilderstein, mock German for "wild man's rock," refers to a petroglyph—probably of Indian Chief Ankony, who ceded the land to Dutch settlers in 1686—that is located at the edge of the cove below the house site.

The Native American petroglyph, c. 1688, that inspired Wilderstein's name. Photograph by Allan Frost of Poughkeepsie, August 1930.

Thomas's family flourished. The marriage was exceptionally happy. Catharine was his "kitten" and his Kate; he was her "dear Tom." On June 5, 1856, they were blessed with a second son, whom they named Robert Bowne after her great uncle, who had established a stationery and general store in New York City in 1775. Their daughter and last child, Kittie, was born on September 18, 1860. Thomas's joy in his children shines forth in a teasing letter from the elder Rutsen. "Now let me know the meaning of those cabal-like letters, TSVP. Do they mean Tom Suckley Vice President or Tom's Son Very Pretty?" It is also reflected in his daybooks which, kept for business, are nonetheless sprinkled with family items—"a wheel barrow for RS, Jr.," "a silver cup for Kittie," and "tuition for Rutsen's school." A charming note from Kate's sister Caroline to young Rutsen when he was four years old speaks of the affectionate visiting back and forth between relatives.

> I was very glad to receive your dear little letter and to hear from you all about home. I understand you went to pay Henry Olin a visit a few days ago and saw his locomotive, but it was too bad that it had no smoke. I have been making little Robert 3 yellow frocks and I should not be surprised if his mama was to give him a pair of little black shoes very soon that dear little brother will learn from Rutsen how to walk, and then how glad he will be... When it gets warm and pleasant and

> you come to see me, we will have a hoop and run about and go in the garden and pick the raspberries. Currants, too. Give little brother a kiss and tell him that Cassie loves both her little boys dearly.

The Civil War did not seem to impinge on the Suckleys' happiness. The railroad made travel to and from New York City easy, and Thomas took advantage of it with fair frequency, for the house on St. Mark's Place remained a family center. Kate sometimes accompanied him to attend the theater and concerts or simply to shop and visit her own aunts and cousins in Brooklyn.

The focus of their lives, however, was Wilderstein. During the summer of 1865, Thomas contemplated an addition to the house. The children were growing and needed more space. That addition never came to be. On December 30, 1865, the twelve-year-old Rutsen was killed in a fall from an apple tree. Wilderstein, the font of so much happiness, became "that desolate dwelling" with appalling suddenness. "I cannot express or speak of my irreparable loss," wrote Kate to her sister-in-law Mary, as she gave sensitive hints on how to speak to Thomas about the tragedy.

Life, of course, continued. At age fourteen, Robert was sent to the Hudson River Institute in Claverack, New York, easily reached by train. His mother wrote him daily. He wrote frequently and returned for vacations. Kittie attended the DeGarmo Insitute in Rhinebeck and briefly went away to boarding school. However, her health was delicate, and she was much at home, where she occupied herself painting watercolors, collecting recipes, and attending to the flower gardens.

Robert entered Wesleyan College in 1874 and graduated in 1878. The college was undoubtedly chosen for him because it had been founded by Methodists and because the Suckleys' neighbor, Stephen Olin, had been president of the institution. There, he became a member of the Alpha Delta Psi fraternity and worried his father by earning demerits for cutting classes and "making noise" in the evenings.

Thomas had far more serious things to worry about. His sister Mary had died in 1872. Rutsen died in 1875. He inherited the greater part of the Suckley fortune, so ably managed under Rutsen's long stewardship, but that did not make up for the void that they left. He had barely adusted to those breaks in the fabric of his life, when death struck again—and again. On January 3, 1879, Kittie succumbed to tuberculosis. Kate, who had been ill the entire previous year, died of grief nine months later. Mary Garrettson also died that year.

Thomas never recovered. Only his love for his remaining child, Robert, mitigated his sorrow. He bought Mary Garrettson's property and rented it to his Hunt cousins, who had a daughter named Grace, a few years younger than Kittie, with whom he formed a tender relationship. Otherwise, Thomas filled his time trying to duplicate Rutsen's meticulous care of the family estate. He gave substantial money to worthy charities, such as the Methodist ministers' retirement home the Suckleys had established on Mt. Rutsen. He took an interest in the neighborhood school and helped needy individuals in imaginative ways. But he became more and more of a recluse, tended by loyal servants.

Elizabeth Philips Montgomery and Robert Bowne Suckley during their courtship. It is not known whether these Rockwood Studio photographs were taken at the same time. If any wedding photographs were made, none has survived.

After he had absorbed the first shock of his sister's and his mother's deaths, Robert spent most of his time in New York City, where he gave his father a hand with his real estate. He bought law books and rented an office with the idea of becoming a lawyer, but he did not study in earnest. Like many young men of his wealthy background, he devoted himself primarily to the strenuous social life of the city. However, like his father before him, he lived on an allowance given him by Thomas rather than on capital of his own.

In 1882, Robert began courting Elizabeth Philips Montgomery. She was just eighteen, and according to one of his aunts, "very young and very sweet." He was twenty-six. Elizabeth's father, Henry Eglinton Montgomery, had been the rector of the fashionable Episcopal Church of the Incarnation in New York City. At his death in 1874 he had left a family of nine children in the hands of a capable and strong-minded widow, but with very little money to support them.

Like Robert, Elizabeth could trace her ancestry to the Beekmans and Livingstons. In fact, her ties were broader and closer. Through her mother, Margaret Augusta Lynch, she could trace her family back to Margaret Beekman Livingston, who had rebuilt that family's seat, Clermont, in Columbia County, following its destruction by the British in 1777. Her great-grandmother was Margaret Livingston Tillotson, whose Linwood estate, although no longer family-owned, overlooked the Hudson just south of

Wilderstein. During the summers, Elizabeth and her family often visited Lynch and Olin relatives at Glenburn, one mile east of Wilderstein and still another slice of the original Livingston grant. It may well be that Robert met Elizabeth at Glenburn, for Henry Olin was a friend from childhood.

The courtship enjoyed the usual zigs and zags. That Robert had become especially close to Elizabeth's brother Lynch, who joined him in a number of ill-starred business dealings as well as in sowing wild oats, may not have helped matters. In October 1882, he sent her a bouquet of beautiful flowers for which she wrote a brief note of thanks, hoping his father was better and closing, "I remain your sincere friend." Early the following June she prissily wrote: "As I have no other engagement to-morrow, I shall be very happy to see you at the time you designate." By the end of that month he had left for a European tour. Lynch saw him off, presenting him with a farewell missive from Elizabeth, who enjoined him to imagine her promenading along the boardwalk at Long Beach, a popular New Jersey seaside resort.

Elizabeth Montgomery self portrait, sent in a letter to Robert Suckley during their courtship; "Drawn by herself" in Bessie's hand; "Nov. 5, 1883," in Robert's hand.

Robert enjoyed the varied pleasures of London, Dublin, and Paris. (His passport lists his occupation as "gentleman.") But, as his travel diary makes clear, the adventure he found most exhilarating was his ascent of Mont Blanc from Chamonix, France. Mountain climbing—indeed, all mountain sports—would become a lifelong passion.

On his return, Elizabeth sent him a little pencil cartoon "of herself, by herself." The expression is worried. A few weeks later, he sent her medicine for a cough. She still had some that he had given her the previous year and she returned it via Lynch, who baldly stated, "Here's the bottle, it's not needed." Robert, stricken by what he took as a rebuff, apologized profusely for having overstepped the privileges of a "long intimacy."

On February 15, 1884—the day after St. Valentine's—Elizabeth heaped more coals on his head. "My dear Mr. Suckley," she wrote, "As I have three important engagements tomorrow which I cannot possibly break I shall have to decline your kind invitation. Very sincerely EHP Montgomery, 49 E. 44th St. I am so sorry." Nothing changed until the end of March. Then something must have snapped, for Robert poured out his heart to her in a love letter. On April 1, at 4:30—quite possibly a.m.—she penned this effusive, confusing letter in reply: "My Cavalier, I have been expecting to see you every day...Have you been thinking of me? It is very sweet of you. You know I must get more used to you before I am very affectionate so you must hurry up and get well so I may see you often.... You must be careful never to catch such another cold for your sake as well as mine... You will always be good won't you? I always want to look up to you, because I feel so small myself and find it so hard to help making mistakes..." Her salutation was "Truly yrs.—Bessie Montgomery."

Then Robert laid his heart on the line. "Dear Miss Bessie," he wrote,

> Yesterday at Rhinebeck I received the most lovely letter that was ever written—a letter that you of all the world, alone could have written. When I try to thank you for it I deeply feel the poverty of words to express the gratitude that is within me, and I can only faintly shadow my sentiments by saying that in it your gentle self appeared, more like, even than ever before, the angel whom I worship and reverence. You cannot now appreciate or understand how you fill my whole heart & mind, how my every thought has you for its center and object, and that the one aim to be attained in my life is your love & trust. So everything you do or say I think and study over afterwards, and, if it seems to point to the possibility of your loving me, I am supremely happy, but if it implies that you are merely pitying, or worse, enduring me, I am like one who has lost all things and whose future is the blackness of loneliness & desolation...

Shortly afterwards, he complained that she treated him coldly. She replied she appreciated his affection and missed him very much, adding that she had had a vivid dream in which he played a prominent part, but found it impossible to tell him about it.

At the end of July she began her "*elaborate* trousseau." She nattered about his health and told him that she had had another dream in which he was so very unkind that again she would not describe it. He sent her candy and books. Apologizing for her lack of charitableness toward mankind, she sent him a four-leaf clover "to ward off more disappointments."

At this point, Bessie's mother intervened. She had reservations about the marriage, if not the romance, and she was frank about them:

> My dear Robert, Since I saw you last evening, I feel more than ever convinced that it will be impossible for me to name the time for the wedding until something is definitely arranged. I could not think of allowing you to assume these new responsibilities while you are still subject to the (shall I say it?) *caprice* of your father, although I would

Bessie and Robert Suckley. Souvenir tintype made during their wedding trip in Europe.

not, for a moment, doubt his generous *intentions.* As the husband of Bessie, I am sure you will agree with me, you could not remain as you are now, in an uncertain position, dependent upon contingencies and I am sure your father will look upon it with the same common-sense point of view.

I write to you, because as you know, it is so difficult to obtain an opportunity for a quiet talk...

Although she could easily measure the depth of the Suckley fortune, Mrs. Montgomery was taking no chances that Thomas would give Robert capital of his own or die soon and solvent.

Some sort of marriage settlement must have been agreed upon. Robert's later daybooks speak of Bessie's money and of borrowing from her funds. At the very least Thomas increased Robert's allowance substantially. The wedding date was set for October 24, 1884 at the Church of the Incarnation.

If anything, Bessie became more nervous as the day approached. Robert was troubled, as well he might have been, by her swift shifts of temper. She must have refused to see him, for on October 12 she wrote him a half-hearted apology: "There is really nothing the matter, but such a drooping and faded plant I am sure you would not like to see." Moreover, she desired that only very near relations and a few intimate friends attend the ceremony. "Scratch out all those cousins," she ordered.

The marriage did take place as planned. For their wedding trip they went to Europe where they stayed for two years, living handsomely on the five thousand dollars a year Thomas had agreed to give them. From time to time, Thomas could not resist cautioning them against extravagance, but otherwise, their correspondence was witty, warm, and frequent. To have a new daughter in Bessie was obviously a great joy to Thomas.

Bessie with her first child, Rutsen, born in Europe, 1885. Cabinet card by Julius Ludovici Studio, New York.

While they were living in Switzerland, their first child, Rutsen, was born. A second was on its way when they returned home in the autumn of 1886. Surprisingly, instead of settling in Rhinebeck with a second home in New York City, they rented a house in Orange, New Jersey, a fashionable and rapidly growing commuting suburb. The house proved impossible to heat—a problem that occasioned many misery-loves-company letters between father and son. Just before the birth of their second son—Henry Eglinton Montgomery, born on February 18, 1887—they bought a larger and better-built house just down the street. It was "exquisite," Robert's cousin, Grace Sands Hunt, sighed in her journal, with turrets, balconies, and beautifully inlaid wood floors, as well as a "dear little conservatory with a fountain." Grace also reported "a very swell dinner" with thirteen courses, after which Robert played the violin, accompanied on the piano by Bessie's oldest sister Nettie. Then, everyone danced. Grace also noted that Robert was stouter and less handsome than before his marriage.

To live in such fine style, Robert needed more money than Thomas was willing to give him. On January 1, 1888, he obtained a franchise from the Heisler Electric Company of St. Louis, Missouri, to use their system of generation and distribution to bring electricity to West Orange. Operations began in May with his brother-in-law Lynch a partner in the venture.

All this activity did not seem to place a barrier between Robert and his father. Robert seldom visited Wilderstein, but he and Thomas continued to meet in the city for pleasure as well as for business. They had such an appointment for February 8. Earlier that week, however, Thomas suffered either a heart attack or a stroke, and all Robert could do was to keep vigil. Thomas Holy Suckley died at Wilderstein the afternoon of February 9.

In a letter consoling him, Bessie, who had remained in New Jersey, wrote:

> My dear Robbie, I am very sorry to hear that sad news. I long to see you that we may talk together over one who has been so good to us. Mamma was saying this morning that such a death was so enviable and we should feel very grateful that his end was so peaceful and without pain. My dear Robbie cannot you send me a few words on paper if you have time. I miss you so much. Lovingly, your wife, Bessie.

On a separate page, she added a bare sentence. "The children are very well."

Christmas 1889. Rutsen and Henry Suckley with their mother and father, their grandmother Montgomery, their cousin Grace Sands Hunt, and their uncles Harry and Alan Montgomery on the west verandah steps. The box on stilts on the right is a rain gauge. Brown exterior paint covers the original polychrome paint scheme which was so flamboyant, it was said to have caused Bessie to faint. It was immediately covered with somber brown.

Cannon, Vaux, Tiffany

1888
1897

THE FACT REMAINED THAT ROBERT now possessed the family fortune. Conservatively estimated, his income was at least six times what it had been. Apparently, Robert never considered remaining in New Jersey, pleasant as was his and Bessie's life there. Within a month, he was making plans to move to Wilderstein, not, however, before the house had undergone radical alterations. With a growing family—a third baby was on its way—he and Bessie desired not only more room, but such conveniences as a working furnace, adequate servants' quarters, and a kitchen on the same floor as the dining room.

They also desired a stylish house. Too plain even for the age in which it was built, Thomas Holy Suckley's austere Italianate villa was hopelessly forlorn when measured by the tastes of the 1880s. For over a decade, the Queen Anne style had been all the rage. First introduced to Americans by the British at the Centennial Exposition in Philadelphia, its genius was to combine the architectural embellishments of earlier ages with a high degree of modern comfort. The principal features of the British residence and office building at the fair were half-timbered gables, glittering banks of windows and a baronial entrance hall, a grand open staircase and cozy nooks. To these, Americans added motifs from their own heritage. The historical ethos stirred up by the Centennial year generated a nostalgia—and new respect—for the generous proportions of late colonial and Federal architecture. These themes were further enlivened by a strong infusion of orientalism. Fascination with the arts and crafts of Persia, India, and China, generated by trade and exploration, was raised to a new pitch by the Exposition's Japanese pavilion and bazaar. However, Queen Anne style eclecticism was not a mindless hodgepodge. Rather it was a springboard into a new, and at its best, a robust expression of individuality. The Suckleys' houses

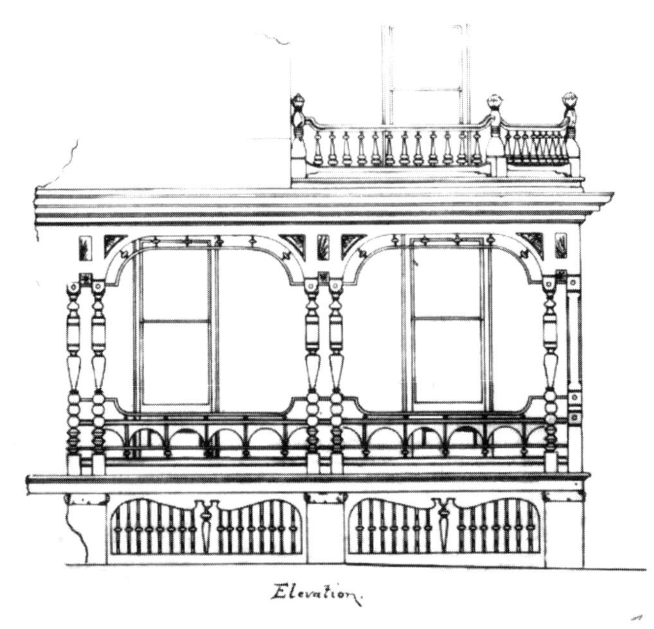

in Orange had given them a taste for the potential of the style. Now they would have a chance to create it on their own.

Since what Robert envisioned was so radically different from his father's austere house, it would not have been surprising if he had elected to tear down the existing structure and thus totally liberate himself from its constraints. His neighbor, Levi P. Morton (that year to become the vice president of the United States), had just done that, replacing William Kelly's Ellerslie with a grand Jacobean "cottage" designed by architect to the very wealthy, Richard Morris Hunt. That Robert chose not to raze his father's villa suggests that he was driven to rewrite rather than obliterate his often melancholy past: when he was just nine years old, he lost his older brother and, as a teen-ager, witnessed his sister's slow decline; and then, in his early twenties, suffered both her and his mother's death in the same year. Moreover, from a practical point of view, saving key structural elements may have been the quickest way of fulfilling the vision that now possessed him.

Whatever the inspiration, Robert must have been thinking about the project for some time, for, within a month of his father's death, he had already secured the services of the ideal architect for his purposes. He was Arnout Cannon, Jr., of Poughkeepsie, New York. Not only a designer, but firmly grounded in structural engineering, Cannon had apprenticed under his father as a mechanic, then studied in New York City with the well-known architect Frederick Diaper. On his return to Poughkeepsie, he joined forces with his brothers Cornelius and George, both of whom were experienced

Above: Arnout Cannon Jr., (1839-1898), architect of the Suckley's Queen Anne style house and carriage house and stable.

Opposite: Detail of verandah embellishments, drawn by architect Arnout Cannon, Jr., 1888. Cannon's verandah with its sweeping southerly view of the Hudson River and its westerly view of the Catskill mountain range became the family's living room from early spring to late fall.

contractors. With them, he built the Vassar Brothers Home for Aged Men, the Vassar Brothers Library, and the Vassar Brothers Institute. He is credited as the architect of the Palatine Hotel in Newburgh as well as the Masonic temple and Nelson House Annex in Poughkeepsie. The house that he designed in that city for steamboat owner John Brinkerhoff still stands. Its striking feature is a sweeping porch with elaborately turned posts and railings.

Cannon was, without question, versatile. Moreover, he was able to assemble a team of first-rate workmen, some of whom had just come off the Ellerslie job or from Crumwold Hall, a medieval-inspired mansion Hunt had designed for Hyde Park resident Archibald Rogers. His managerial capability was honed during the Civil War when he was a commander of negro troops. These talents were essential, not only because Robert and Bessie insisted the alteration go swiftly, but also because, fascinated by new technologies, Robert would contract the heating, plumbing and electricity himself.

By the first of May, 1888, Cannon had completed drawings that reflected Robert's desires. So radical was the transformation that it is difficult to believe the basic structure was retained. Simply, the verandahs were extended and profusely decorated. For dramatic effect as well as for practical purposes, the small porch leading to the principal entrance was replaced with an imposing porte cochere whose pyramidal roof, culminating in a huge egg-shaped finial, resembles a royal oriental umbrella. The Tuscan roof was taken off and the walls raised with an overhanging third story and gabled attic. The steeply pitched new roof was covered with red slate. Still, it was supported by brackets of the same design as those for the villa; some were, perhaps, salvaged from it. The ridge lines carried crenelations of tin. The gutters were enclosed in box cornices. All four chimneys were raised high above the roof and two more were added. They were red brick and corbelled at the top.

But what gave the new Wilderstein its unique character was its soaring five-story tower. Fitted into the north end of the western facade, it is a glittering confection of glass and fancy paneling. Its roof is a jaunty, peaked "candle snuffer" cone, embellished by an iron finial with sunflowers at its base, scrollwork to designate the compass points midway up, and a small crown of flames at the top. Virtually invisible from the east and south lawns, this exuberant tower comes as a glorious surprise to a first visitor. But from the river, it is what distinguished Wilderstein from all other mansions along its banks. The tower also solved a practical design problem. It serves as a buffer between the family part of the house and the spacious two-story-and-attic servants' wing added to the north end.

To tie this giddy upward explosion to the land, Cannon extended the verandah to embrace all but the north side of the house. Its half-circle bays are ornamented with carved sunbursts, rosettes, and quill-like decorations. The railings are a parade of arcs and fancifully turned spindles. Used as an informal family gathering place from early spring through the fall and even on balmy days in winter, its wide-roofed spaces join the house to the landscaped lawn, so that it seems to rise naturally out of the land.

INTERIORS

The alterations to the interior of the 1852 villa were equally exhaustive. The drawing room was retained and the dining room, to which a bay was added, became the parlor. The south bedrooms remained as bedrooms. But everything else was radically changed. A great hall and staircase, so essential to the Queen Anne home, was fitted into the space formerly occupied by the entrance hall and office. The dining room—replacing the old hall, stair, and butler's pantry—was enlarged by the semicircular bay formed by the tower's base. A door was cut into the north wall, leading to the new pantry, kitchen, and butler's office.

On the second floor, the north bedroom was eliminated by the new stairwell. Its one-and-a-half-story-high three-paneled window of pastel-tinted "cathedral glass" does much to illuminate the interior halls, as well as the stairs. The northwest bedroom, which Suckley would take for his own, was enlivened by the tower bay. The family bathroom was removed to the servants' wing.

Above: The short-lived water tower in disguise, c. 1892. The plants along the base of the verandah are elephant ears.

Below: Wilderstein with awnings and its third coat of paint — cream with brown trim, 1905. In 1910, the Suckley's gave Wilderstein its last coat of paint — plain brown. Restoration of the 1889 polychrome palette began in 1994.

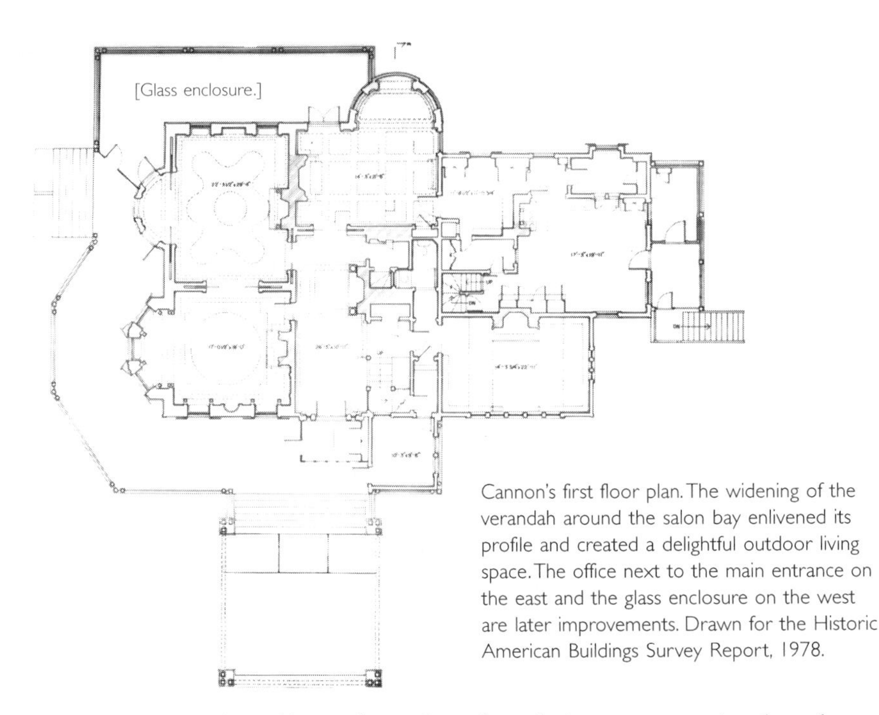

Cannon's first floor plan. The widening of the verandah around the salon bay enlivened its profile and created a delightful outdoor living space. The office next to the main entrance on the east and the glass enclosure on the west are later improvements. Drawn for the Historic American Buildings Survey Report, 1978.

The cellar of the villa, with its firm foundations, was retained, and was considerably enlarged by the tower and service wing. Because of the downward slope of the land, the windows on the westerly side are double size, making the laundry installed there a pleasant place to work.

Robert was pleased with Cannon's design. Presented with a choice between a round tower and an octagonal one, he quickly chose the round even though it was several hundred dollars more expensive. The minor changes he requested were, Cannon cheerfully wrote, "very easy to make." Work started immediately. In fact, the mason had been on the job since the middle of April. In early June the carpenters were framing and Cannon was pressing Robert to give him the name of his plumber so that the iron drain from the cesspool to the inside of the basement could be laid.

As he was still living in New Jersey and was occupied with managing his real estate and launching his electric company, Robert's visits to the site were sporadic and brief. Usually he came up only for the day. But his confidence in Cannon proved justified. Progress was so steady that Cannon felt free to repair to Coney Island for a brief holiday. Shortly after his return he was ready to discuss exterior painting, which, he advised, was easier to do while the scaffolding was still up. The last week of August, Cannon was able to report that the chimneys were underway, the roof slating complete, and the lightning rods installed.

CARRIAGE HOUSE AND STABLE

Designing, contracting, and supervising so speedy a transformation of Wilderstein was a remarkable architectural and engineering feat in itself, but, at the same time, Cannon was designing a carriage house and stable, as well as a boat house for the property. He was also responsible for the construction of the road that would connect them. A job-seeking Hyde Park workman captured the atmosphere perfectly. "I understand," he wrote Cannon, "that you are doing a big lot of work at Wilderstein."

To a great extent, Cannon had been confined by the dictates of the original structure. Now he was free to make a unique statement. Suckley, who was in the process of acquiring a six-seat rockaway, a three spring wagonette, a two-seat wagon, a "T" cart, a donkey cart, and a six-passenger Russian *vis-a-vis,* had only one requirement—that the building housing them and his horses be handsome and large. Dramatically sited on the edge of a ravine, down hill and slightly north of the house, the carriage house and stable is Queen Anne at its best. A huge onion-shaped dome—capping for a disguised ventilator—dominates the massive slate-clad roof. It is topped by a striding horse weather vane, the famous trotter "Black Hawk." A small octagonal tower, decorated with metal flowers, and a cupola, adorned by botanical cattails—also ventilator caps—render the roof line still more lively. The building's profile, seen against the background of the river and the mountains beyond, is at once fanciful, ingenious and majestic.

.View of the carriage house and stable from the west lawn. When she first saw the majestic building, Robert's cousin Grace exclaimed, "I quite envy the horses their sumptuous quarters." Note Calvert Vaux 's 1890 gazebo beyond Catharine Bowne Suckley's 1852 garden. Several of the cedar trees marking the brink of the ravines still exist. Snapshot taken by Robert Suckley, c. 1890, using an early hand-held Kodak camera of the kind introduced by George Eastman in 1888.

The textures of the exterior are masterfully orchestrated. The diamond patterns of the slate clad roof, the fish-scale shingles, the patterned brick, the rusticated and smooth-cut stone and the wooden doors catch the light in constantly changing ways. Fanlights and gables, spindles and sunbursts mirror those embellishing the house. The splendid three-quarter relief carving of a horse's head and the immense rusticated stone and corbelled brick chimney inset with two terracotta plaques, one bearing Suckley's monogram "RBS," the other, the date "'88," lend the building an intimate touch. It is hard to believe that it covers some four thousand square feet of land and contains ten thousand square feet of usable space. Cousin Grace Hunt's reaction to its splendor put it nicely: "I quite envy the horses their sumptuous quarters."

R. Alex Decker, a builder from Rhinebeck, and Henry W. Otis, a mason from Kingston, joined forces and with a bid of $16,000 won the contract to erect this lordly structure. They promised to begin on August 1, 1888, and to finish by November 1. Decker and Otis did not quite meet their deadline; but, on December 8, the stable fixtures had arrived and Decker had started putting in the gutters.

BOAT HOUSE AND ICE HOUSE

Little was done to the ice house that lay between the main house and the carriage house. For esthetic reasons Robert might have moved it a little to the north, but he left it exactly where his father had placed it. It was the oldest structure on the place. Later he would say that in his youth he had used it first as a play house and then as a shop, presumably in the months it

The boathouse, although plainer, was ornamented to match the main buildings.

was emptied of ice. Simply, the roof was slated and a few decorative elements added to the facade to give it a character similar to the house.

Suckley's father had never developed the waterfront at Wilderstein, but by the 1880's, boating had become a fashionable sport. Among Robert's first purchases when he inherited Wilderstein was a thirty-foot naptha-powered launch, named *Ellide*. Made of mahogany, she had silver chocks and cleats, leather cushions, and a small-figured carpet. He also ordered an iceboat, to be called *Dombey*, a pet name for his son Henry. She was made by the renowned shipbuilder Jacob E. Buckhout of Poughkeepsie. In addition, he bought a skiff and contemplated a sailing catamaran. For this expanding fleet, he asked Cannon to design a boat house. It was to be located on a small parcel of land, west of the railroad tracks and adjacent to the Ellerslie dock, on which he had procured a long lease from the New York Central and Hudson River Railroad.

On August 8, 1888, Cannon presented the desired plans. The boat house was rectangular in shape with the slip opening toward the south in deference to current, tide, and prevailing winds. Stairs at the side of the slip led to the main floor, an open loft space with a polygonal dressing room skewed in one corner. As with the carriage house and stable, Cannon used exterior details such as fish-scale shingles to render it compatible in style with the house.

Buckhout sought the contract to build this structure. The work was given to Cannon's brother Cornelius. Nevertheless, Buckhout did not hesitate to advise. When he told Robert the balcony must be shortened if the larger boats were to be launched in the slip, the balcony was shortened. Buckhout also built the floating ramp that, rising and falling with the tide, made it convenient to board the boats at any time of day.

Throughout the summer, contractors had used the Ellerslie dock for delivery of building materials. Although the road leading to it ran along Wilderstein's north boundary, the grade was so precipitous that the heavy loads put a terrible strain on the horses. In any case, Robert wanted his own approach from the river. Like the outbuildings, he expected it to be picturesque as well as functional.

Cannon engaged T. F. Lawler, a civil engineer and the proprietor of the Manhattan Bridge Building Company, to do the survey. The road he laid out starts at the railroad track directly inland from the Indian rock—the "wilderstein." After a short, relatively steep ascent, it sweeps southeast almost parallel to the river, then, traversing in a narrow loop, climbs to the carriage house, an elevation of sixty feet. On December 1, Lawler wrote Robert that the work was "done as well as could be considering the weather."

All he wanted was a little freeze to set the culverts. Proud of his achievement, he complained that Robert had not made time to inspect his work on that day, when he had been up from the city.

Robert's inaccessibility was not due to indifference, but rather to focus. During this period he had been directing the design, purchase, and installation of the heating, burglar alarm, and bell systems for the house. The alarm system had an indicator with a clock and a disconnect device. The bell system included a five-inch gong that posted the source of the call—the library, parlor, drawing room, or his bedroom. (Orders from Bessie's southwest bedroom were conveyed to the butler's pantry by means of a speaking tube.) In October, a telephone line, earlier installed in the house, was run from the house to the stable.

Contemporary photographs and recent paint analysis suggest that the house was first painted light apricot brown with contrasting dark reddish brown trim and bronze green sashes, and that the background of the imitation half-timbering was painted putty color to look like stucco. A family legend relates that Bessie fainted when she saw the "garish manner" in which the polychrome emphasized the decorative detail. In any case, shortly afterwards, the color scheme was changed to a more subdued reddish brown with dark brown trim.

JOSEPH BURR TIFFANY'S ROOMS

So far, what Cannon had produced was a handsome shell. The sumptuous wood paneling, plaster ceilings, parquet floors, mantelpieces, wall coverings, stained-glass windows, and suitable furnishings had still to be designed. Abandoning his hands-on approach, Robert entrusted this work to Joseph Burr Tiffany of New York City, a specialist in the burgeoning field of interior decoration.

Trained in architecture and engineering at Cornell, and for some time afterward connected with the art department of his uncle's Union Square emporium Tiffany and Company, Joseph Burr Tiffany had recently started a decorating business of his own, with offices at 12 East 22nd Street, just off Fifth Avenue at the north end of what was called the "Ladies' Mile." "While carrying no stock," his announcement in the April 1888 issue of *Decorator and Furnisher* read, "they have at all times a large variety of samples, from which designs and color may be suggested or selected." Tiffany had as yet no previous large commissions to show the quality of his work. However, he came with a strong letter of recommendation from the Reverend Bishop Falkner of St. Mark's Rectory in Orange, New Jersey. An episcopal prelate, he very well may have been Bessie's candidate.

Tiffany and Robert commenced discussions in mid-October and by Thanksgiving Robert had preliminary drawings and specifications in hand. The hall, staircase and dining room were to be in the English Jacobean style; the library in the Flemish medieval style; the drawing room in the style of Louis XVI; and the parlor—Tiffany refers to it as "the morning room"—"delicately paneled" American colonial. Tiffany's special darling was a painted and gilded conservatory opening off the base of the tower on the west side of the dining room. The whole was the quintessential Queen Anne amalgam, endorsed by the American Institute of Architects and by thousands of homeowners, great and small.

Above: Joseph B. Tiffany's drawing of the Jacobean style dining room's overmantel, 1888.

Right: Tiffany penciled an elaborate sconce, capable of being electrified, onto the original ink drawing.

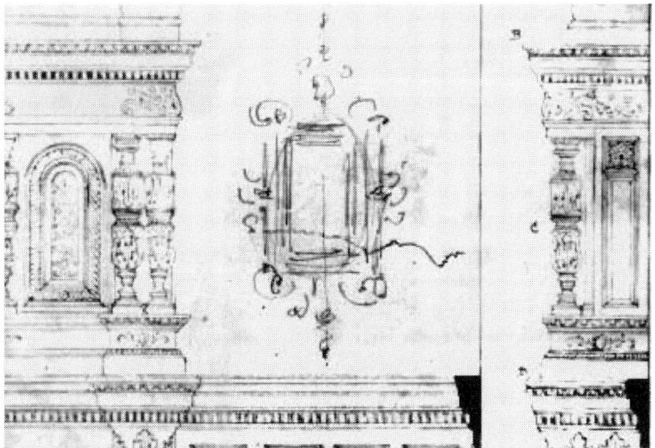

Robert vetoed the conservatory and insisted the work be completed in four months. Experienced enough to know that coordinating with the builders might cause annoying delays, Tiffany made a hurried trip to Rhinecliff to talk with Cannon about scheduling. Finally, on Christmas Eve 1888, he delivered a new set of specifications, accompanied by a cost estimate that Robert could accept, $36,600. A princely sum—more than four times Cannon's structural costs—it did not include rough carpentry, masonry, brickwork, plastering, wiring, plumbing or heating. Moreover, Robert was to assume responsibility for problems arising from acts or omissions committed by workmen and other parties employed.

Tiffany's job was to provide "all hardware and cabinet finishing, all metal work, mirrors, glass work, marble and tile and stone work, all decorations executed in plaster, stucco, onyx, oil color, leather, tapestry or silk, leaving the ground floor complete and ready to receive such furniture, curtains, carpets etc. as the Suckleys would provide." He also promised wrought-iron andirons for the dining room and parlor, stained glass windows for the hall and the dining room, a candelabra for the salon, which was to be lighted with candles, and gas light fixtures for the rest of the house. (Apparently, at the outset Robert did not confide that he was planning to have electric light in many of the rooms.)

In a series of loose descriptions rather than detailed specifications, Tiffany stated that the hall and stairway, including the hall floor, were to be executed in quartered oak, the hall walls to be covered in stamped leather. Mahogany would be used throughout the dining room, including the immense overmantle and the ceiling, the floor and the built-in buffet. The woodwork in the parlor would be light cherry, the walls hung with silk tapestry, the ceiling embellished with a delicate flowery design. For the library, a room Tiffany had urged Cannon to wedge in west of the grand staircase, he chose quartered oak wainscoting and bookcases. The salon was to be a fantasy in white and gold painted woodwork, its ceiling elaborately decorated, its walls covered with silk damask. Since the entire floor was to be covered with a carpet, woven at Robert's expense, it was given no special treatment.

Robert exhibited a great deal of faith in signing this contract, for the drawings that accompanied it were sketchy at best. Although there is no indication Bessie participated actively, the fact that the griffin of the Montgomery coat of arms adorns the dining room's elaborate overmantle and griffins form the basis of andiron and lighting fixture designs, suggests Tiffany was courting her favor, if, indeed, he was not rewarding her for it. However, on September 1, 1888, she had given birth to their third son, Robert Bowne,

ENTRANCE HALL

STAIRCASE THROUGH TO LIBRARY

LIBRARY

DINING ROOM

BUTLER'S PANTRY

WHITE AND GOLD ROOM

PARLOR

SOUTH VERANDAH

Above: Tiffany specified these classic bronze knobs with reed motif for all but two of the first floor doors. On several of them, the shaft is slightly offset to prevent banging knuckles on the jam when twisting.

Below: Tiffany chose more elaborate knobs and plates for the doors in the dining room leading to the butler's pantry and the closet beside it. Photographs by Tom Daley, 1999.

Jr.—he would be called Robin—and, even with nursemaids, managing three children three years old and under, and the large Orange, New Jersey, house would have been a full time job.

Tiffany and his assistant, Mr. Oakley, who would superintend the work, journeyed to Wilderstein immediately after the New Year to talk with Cannon about how to mesh their labors. Since it was apparent Cannon was behind in his plastering, Tiffany told Robert he would do it, but at an additional cost of $650, Robert providing the materials and scaffolding. For another $300 he volunteered to finish the second floor plastering, thus protecting the new plaster below from careless pounding on the floors above. Robert agreed.

Then, probably with support from Cannon, Robert raised questions about the adequacy of Tiffany's drawings and specifications. In his firm reply, Tiffany laid down some truths about the precarious nature of renovating. As the work "involves old as well as the new construction," he wrote, "the specific instructions given from time to time as they are needed are much more valuable than any specifications in the usual form can possibly be. In fact, in such a case as this, it is the only practical way of specifying the work *viz.* to meet each contingency as it arises." Agreeing to specify in advance if Robert insisted, he warned that "no provisions can properly be made to cover the questions arising from the concealed construction of the old building and in those instances we should have to resort to our present method."

Despite minor grumbling, Robert was happy enough with Tiffany's progress to pay him five thousand dollars at the end of January, ten thousand dollars in the middle of February, and five thousand dollars on the first of April. However,

Left: Tiffany's Louis XVI white and gold salon before the Pottier and Stymus furnishings arrived. Taken by Robert B. Suckley with an early hand-held camera, the lens of which did not fill a rectangular frame. Because the level of technology made it so difficult to photograph interiors, this picture displays a highly adventurous spirit.

Opposite: Rutsen and Henry with baby Robin enjoying a jaunt through the Wilderstein property. The name of the long-lived donkey was Jennie.

he did not soften in respect to the May 1, 1889, deadline, and, on April 10, Tiffany was forced to plead with him to prod Cannon into action. "Our carpenters are patiently waiting for your carpenters to level your floors to receive our new hardwood floors," he scolded. "The necessity for this we explained to you personally when you last called upon us."

It did not seem possible that Tiffany would meet his deadline. Not only was there no central heating during the winter, but, in the spring, the west side of the house was constantly disturbed by the installation of a windmill just ten feet from the tower. (Its purpose was to provide the new Wilderstein with a copious, dependable supply of water.) Yet, precisely on May 1, he notified Robert that he had withdrawn his employees and removed all implements from the house and had delivered the keys to Mr. Cannon.

For the most part, Tiffany did just what he contracted to do, and more. The elaborate wood paneling is of the first quality and, after over a century, is as fresh and true as the day it was installed. He supplied a wrought iron winged griffin to hold up the stairway's newel post light and, when Suckley informed him he intended to have electricity, he found a chandelier for the morning room and sconces for the hall that could be electrified. It was he who inspired Cannon to balance the bay window in the salon with one in the parlor. The extra contribution he prized most, however, was the substitution of a large circular painting for the decorative plaster ceiling in the salon. It was by H. Siddons Mowbray, who had painted a mural for the New York Athletic Club and would later win commissions for the University

Club and the Morgan Library in New York City and the Vanderbilt mansion in Hyde Park. Depicting three sprightly cherubs playing with doves among pink cumulus clouds, it gives the room an airy loftiness the plaster ceiling would have lacked. He also placed extra stained glass windows in the hall and stairwell. Executed in rippled, crumpled, striated, and faceted opalescent glass, with a motif resembling a giant moth, they are a triumph. The stained glass he set in the three Tudoresque library windows has the explosive impact of fireworks.

At the end of August, Suckley gave Tiffany his final payment, $9,700.

FURNISHINGS

A stub in Suckley's 1889 checkbook states: "Orange Furniture to Rhinebeck." The teal blue brocade and crushed velvet sofa and chairs, matched by Tiffany in the fireplace tiles and the porcelain vases of its mantel, and the darker blue in the Chinese rug he had selected, gave the morning room a wonderful warmth. The rest of their furniture fit the house so well, too, that their only major expenditure for furnishings was for the white and gold salon.

There is no record of when Bessie, the children, and the servants moved

in, but on March 31, Robert sent a telegram from Rhinecliff to New York, summoning Mrs. Lincoln, the midwife, to Wilderstein. On April 1, 1890. Bessie delivered their fourth son, Arthur Rutsen Lynch. "B. and the baby are very well," Robert remarked in his journal. What is surprising about the event is the baby's name. Arthur was new to both the Suckley and Montgomery families; Rutsen was a repeat, Lynch only is understandable in the context of family tradition. Why they did not choose Thomas or even George for this fourth son is a mystery.

On April 3, Robert ran his new stone crusher for a few moments. Finding its foundation was not "stiff enough," he had it braced against the house. It must have made a terrible racket and probably shook the house, but that did not stop him. Two days later, he triumphantly recorded, it crushed a cubic yard of stone in eighteen minutes. Not content with that achievement, he arranged to buy water rights on the nearby Landsman Kill in order to install a power plant and water system to serve the Wilderstein property.

It might be quipped that Robert produced projects with the same regularity that Bessie produced babies. The truth, however, was probably that, deep within the clubman and sport was a mechanic with a strong inventive streak. The Suckley talent for entrepreneurial adventure seems to have blossomed in Robert in this way. At this time, he subscribed to *Scientific American* and *Popular Mechanics* and bought texts on road building and applied mechanics. His approach to new modes of doing things was not merely theoretical; it was hands-on work.

Perhaps as a present to Bessie, he asked her help in choosing the furniture for Tiffany's Louis XVI drawing room. It took some time for them to make up their minds. Having successfully beaten down the original price, they finally ordered from the stylish Pottier and Stymus a table and two cabinets with white and gold trim and onyx tops; two white and gold ladies' chairs, three gilt reception chairs; a carved sofa and a Louis XVI arm chair, both upholstered with Aubusson-style tapestry; silk damask draperies for the windows, and a pair of plush portieres for the sliding door between the drawing and morning rooms. They also ordered a custom designed wall-to-wall Aubusson carpet through a Boston firm. The furniture would not be delivered until May 1891, the carpet until the fall of that year. They obviously thought them worth waiting for.

After a tour of the new Wilderstein with Robert, Grace Hunt wrote in her journal, "I have always had my idea of a pretty house and the kind of house I have hoped someday to have, but this exceeds even my wildest dream... The old house is hardly recognizable—so many changes, additions etc. have been made...each room seems more beautiful than the other... It is so nice to have money and Robert means to make the most of his, lucky boy."

LANDSCAPING

With his building projects completed, Robert proceeded to focus his creative energies on landscaping. On April 19, 1890, Calvert Vaux and his son Downing came up from New York City to view the grounds and find out in what ways Robert cared to improve them.

There was no more distinguished landscape firm in the United States than Vaux & Company. Calvert Vaux had been a partner of Andrew Jackson Downing and, with him, had laid out the great Washington, D.C. park between the Capitol, the Smithsonian Institution, and the White House. After Downing's death in 1852, Vaux had carried on his forceful tradition, both in landscape design and in architecture. It was Vaux who initiated the design competition for Central Park in New York City and persuaded Frederick Law Olmsted to join him in developing the winning "Greensward" plan. Together, they created many of the enduring urban parks in the United States.

Calvert Vaux
(1839-1895)

Calvert Vaux was the author of *Villas and Cottages*, first published in 1857, a volume of fifty house plans that was of unparalleled influence in his lifetime and is still prized today. He was the first architect for the Metropolitan Museum of Art and the Museum of Natural History in New York City. Frederic E. Church, the renowned Romantic painter, asked for his help in designing Olana, with its panoramic view of the Hudson River valley. Vaux's myriad commissions in the valley gave him familiarity with the natural features Wilderstein possessed. At sixty-five years of age, he was still vigorous and, to back him up, he had his able son Downing and the architect George K. Radford, an Englishman who had been his partner for many years.

Calvert and Downing Vaux's first visit to Wilderstein was successful in every way. They agreed that while they would do the design, Robert would oversee as much of its implementation as possible. "The usual routine of practice when superintendance is undertaken," Calvert told Suckley, "is to

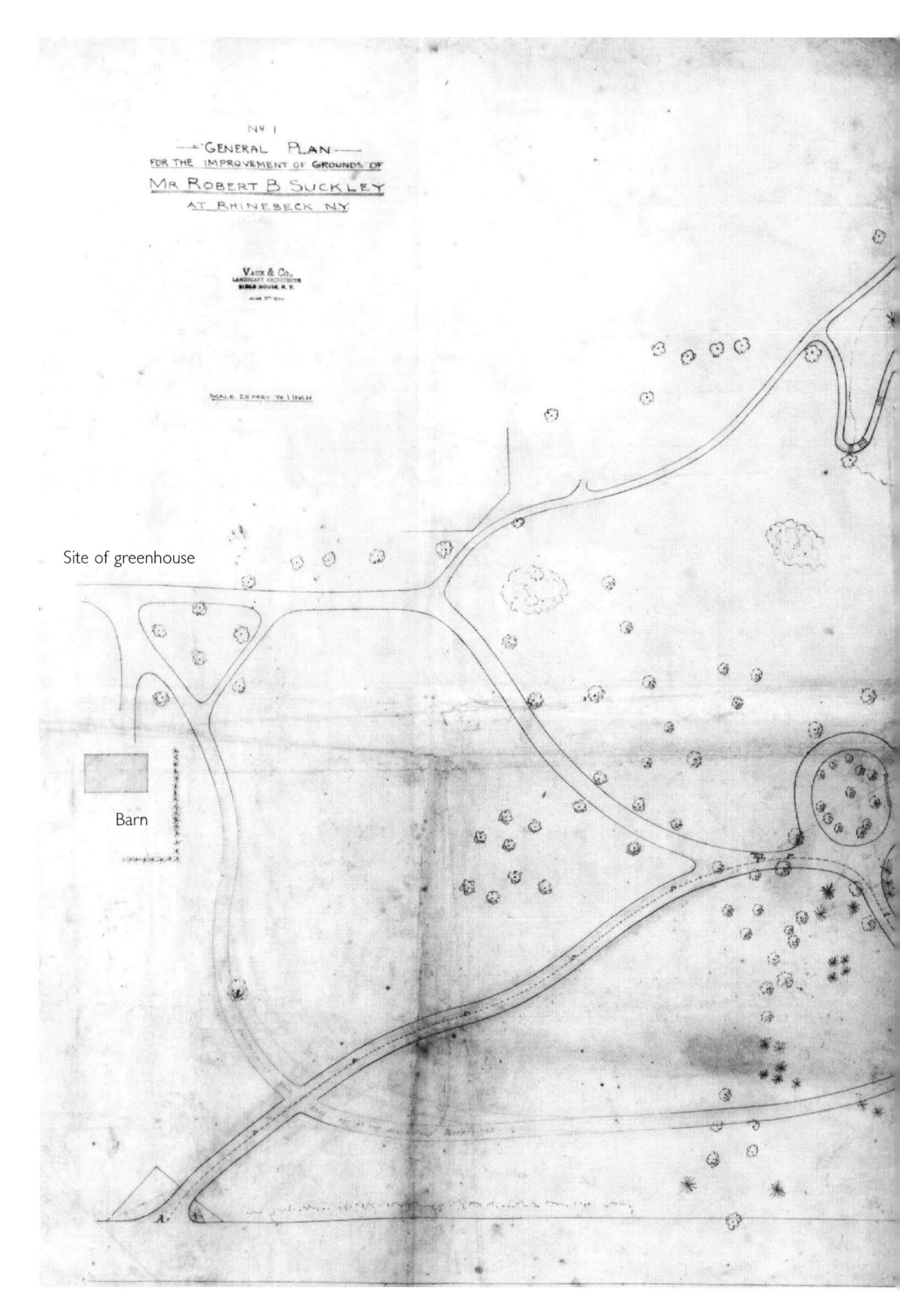
No 1
GENERAL PLAN
FOR THE IMPROVEMENT OF GROUNDS OF
MR ROBERT B SUCKLEY
AT RHINEBECK NY
Vaux & Co.
Site of greenhouse
Barn

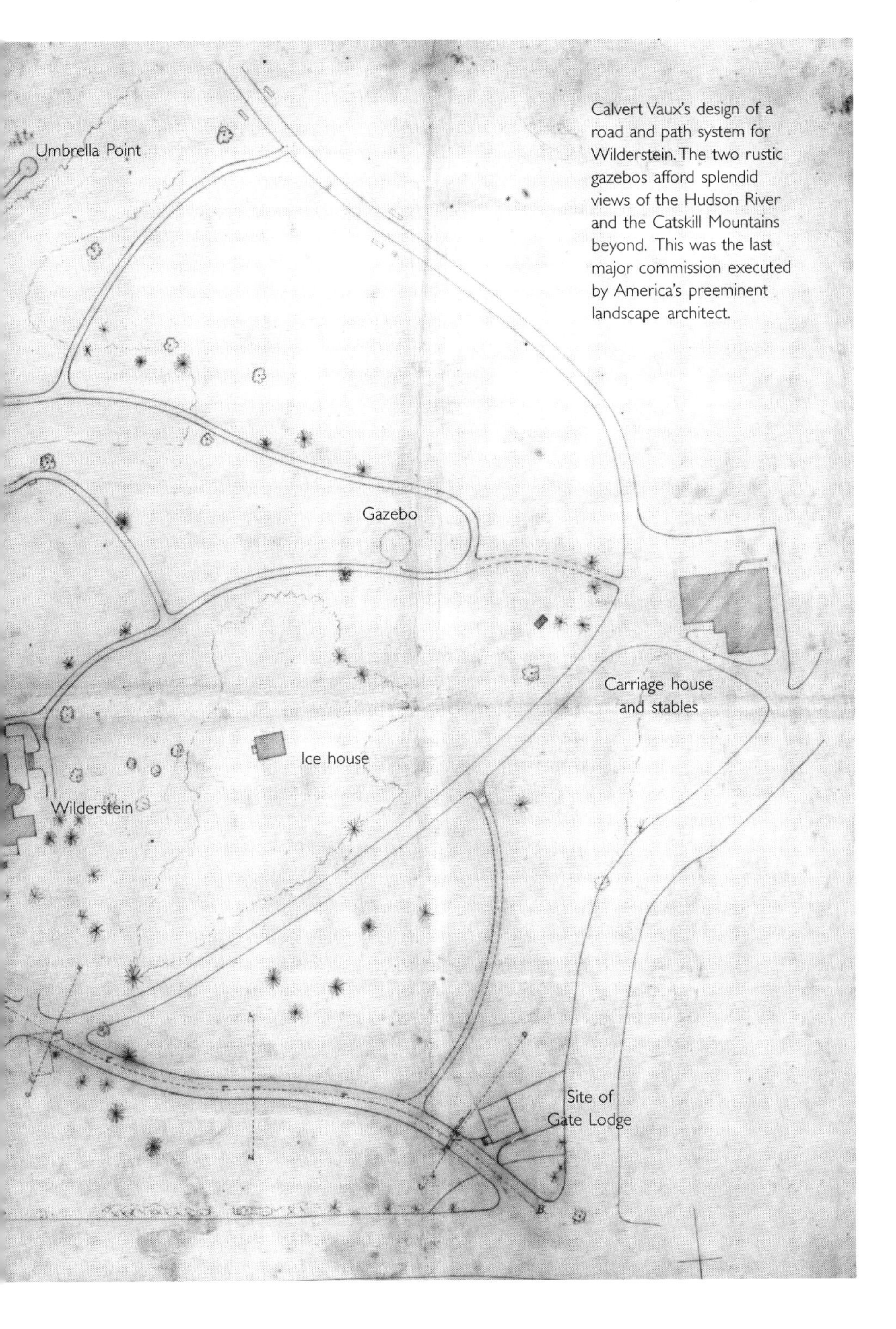

Calvert Vaux's design of a road and path system for Wilderstein. The two rustic gazebos afford splendid views of the Hudson River and the Catskill Mountains beyond. This was the last major commission executed by America's preeminent landscape architect.

"My desire is to get a varied skyline without complexity in the floor plans," Downing Vaux wrote Robert of his design for the Gate Lodge. Stableman Charles Halley, his wife, and his children are seated on the steps in this photograph taken shortly after it was completed.

follow up the issue of such a plan with visits repeated as often as may be required and costing the owner say $10.00 per day and expenses...With your special knowledge, it would be expedient that you should supervise the work yourself at the outset as you could always let us know if any difficulty arose and we could send some one to meet it."

In June 1890, Calvert Vaux sent Robert a design in the Romantic tradition for the road and walk system. Existing interior roads to neighboring Wildercliff and to the carriage house and boat house are preserved. A new narrow road loops in a semicircle across the east lawns to the cutting gardens, and an interlacing of descending walks crisscrosses the bluffs. There is an octagonal gazebo on the knoll between the carriage house and the house and another on the promontory below the house known as "Umbrella Point." Both offer splendid views of the river and mountains.

While the working drawings were being prepared for the grounds, Robert asked Downing Vaux to think about a Gate Lodge, to be lived in by his head grounds man. Vaux replied: "My desire is to get a varied skyline without the complexity in the floor plans."

The Gate Lodge was a two-story house with a hipped gable and a banded and corbelled chimney. The interior was divided into a conventional kitchen, living room, and dining room below and three small bedrooms upstairs. "We have omitted the plumbing," Downing Vaux explained, "as we were not informed as to the question of water and drainage. This part of the work can be added during construction."

THE GREENHOUSE AND POWERHOUSE

To have a greenhouse was the mark of a fine estate in the 1880s. None were considered more elegant than those developed by the Irvington-on-Hudson firm of Lord and Burnham. Robert contacted them in mid-March 1890, and the company recommended that he examine the greenhouse they had built twelve years previously for Ferncliff, the nearby Astor estate, keeping in mind that their system was now very much improved. Suckley inspected and liked it. Soon afterwards, Lord and Burnham submitted a proposal for a greenhouse eighty-two and a half feet long and twenty feet wide. They also sent a rendering of a conservatory to be attached to the dining room as Tiffany had intended. Suckley again rejected the conservatory, but contracted for the greenhouse. The cost was $3,850, including the heating and ventilating apparatus, but not the foundations or plumbing. The potting shed was designed in the Flemish style. In keeping with the emerging vogue, Robert changed it to American colonial.

During the early summer of 1890, while they were waiting for the greenhouse to be fabricated, the family at Wilderstein was busy, happy, and productive. Bessie and Robert called on the Astors, Mortons, and Merritts, neighbors with substantial estates. Robert's Bowne aunts came for extended visits. Bessie's relatives, summering at Glenburn, paid frequent calls. Baby Arthur was gaining weight nicely. All agreed the long, hot days at Wilderstein were idyllic. Then, suddenly, on the night of August 2, young Rutsen was "taken sick with nausea and throwing up." On August 5, he died. Grace Hunt described the tragedy. "Robert's oldest child, dear little Rutsen, died after a very short illness. He had such sweet ways that everyone loved him even to the work people on the place. It was very touching and very beautiful to hear them talk of him and recall his quaint ways and speeches. Just at an age to be companionable, Robert fairly idolized him and it has broken his heart... The funeral was the saddest I ever knew. As I looked at our little dead boy, lying white and still and beautiful among his favorite flowers, I felt as if I was looking at one of God's angels."

For a space, there are no entries in Robert's journal. When they resume, they consist mainly of records of little Arthur's diet and weight. Still, the work on the place went forward. In early November, boxes of greenhouse parts began to arrive. Except for the potting shed, it was finished that month.

However, the project that had the most power to divert Robert's mind from his great sorrow was the building of the power plant. With a dynamo procured through the Heisler Electric Company, it was designed to serve

not only Wilderstein, but also Wildercliff. On January 12, 1891, at 9:00 p.m. Wilderstein's electric lights flashed on. It was a momentous occasion for every inhabitant of the area, as well as for the Suckleys. The first electricity in the United States had been installed in New York City, only nine years before. In rural areas, it was regarded as a miracle.

FINAL IMPROVEMENTS

Despite the excitement of having an electrified country house, the Suckleys spent much of their time in New York City that winter, taking advantage of the extraordinarily frequent train service provided by the New York Central and Hudson River Railroad. They also visited Bessie's relatives who had bought their former house in Orange, New Jersey. Especially for Bessie, it became a haven. When Nummie, as Henry was now called, came down with scarlet fever, Arthur and his nurse were sent there to avoid contagion.

Their trips to Wilderstein were sporadic during the cold weather and had much of the aura of camping out, for the heating system with which Robert had taken so much trouble was not yet working perfectly. On January 21, 1891, he noted in his journal that he and Bessie cooked their supper over the library fire. What drew Robert to Wilderstein most often was the iceboating. He had a standing order with the telegraph operator in Rhinecliff to wire him whenever other boats were out so he could catch the next

Opposite: View along the parterre, terminating with the neo-Colonial potting shed and greenhouse. Roses border the east side of the gravel path. Snapshot taken by Robert B. Suckley, c. 1895.

Above: The glassed area of the Lord and Burnham greenhouse was divided into three sections, so that each could be kept at a different temperature: roses from 50 to 55 degrees, vegetables and other flowers from 55 to 60 degrees, and the vinery from 60 to 65 degrees. Robert proudly complained that the chrysanthemums he entered in the Annandale flower show cost at least five dollars a blossom to grow. Lord and Burnham drawing with Flemish-style potting shed, 1890.

train. It was an exciting sport, with boats clocked at over sixty miles an hour. One windy morning, he noted in his diary, he put his brothers-in-law, Harry and Alan, on the runner planks to steady the boat, and used his farmer, Chester Ramsay, as ballast. By May, however, the whole family was again comfortably settled at Wilderstein. Pottier and Stymus delivered the Louis XVI white-and-gold furniture. The Aubusson carpet was being woven. Both Robert and Bessie were pleased with their elegant surroundings.

Still, Robert was restless without an architectural project in progress and he called upon Downing Vaux to draw up plans for an office to be fitted into the verandah north of the front entrance. He wanted—and, perhaps Bessie insisted on his having—a special room, such as had existed in his father's house, where he could consult with workmen without invading the family quarters. Such an addition would darken one of the beautiful stained glass windows that shed such a beguiling light in the great hall and would interrupt the flow of the verandah. Downing tried to minimize the latter problem by attaching the dismantled railing and ornamental screenwork to the office wall to suggest continuity of the verandah, but it was at best a

(Left to right) Bessie, Robin, Margaret Augusta Lynch Montgomery, Henry, Aunt Nettie, Arthur and Robert, late summer 1891. Of the many copies of this photograph, this is the only one in which the figure of Bessie has not been cut away. A probable explanation is that she edited it because it was considered indelicate to be photographed while obviously pregnant. Their first daughter, Margaret, would be born in December.

lame solution. Robert also hoped to continue the stairwell to the attic and convert part of the space under the eaves into bedrooms. (Another baby was on its way.) Vaux took measurements and drew plans. However, when it came to commissioning the attic work, Robert uncharacteristically held back.

One reason may have been that Robert was beginning to feel he had already spent too much money. A laconic note in his journal of January 1891 states: "an impairment of capital of $1971.64." Another reason may have been that he was busy devising a disguise for his windmill. The versatile Cannon fashioned false windows with shutters for the first and second stories together with siding and decorative panels to match the tower. The windmill never proved successful and, sometime in the 1890s, it was taken down.

Meanwhile, work went briskly forward on the grounds. On March 17, 1891 Calvert Vaux delivered his planting map. The species called for included "299 spirea (three varieties), 150 barberry (two varieties), 74 quince,

10 redbud, 91 dogwood (two varieties), 121 mock orange, 66 forsythia, 64 elderberry, 38 deutzia, 10 stuartia, 4 andromeda, 28 viburnum, and 32 dwarf horse chestnuts." In addition, there were crab apple, willow, ginkgo, birch, purple beech, linden, American elm, sugar maple and regular horse chestnut trees. "The selection," the specifications instructed, "was to be made from trees & shrubs that have been frequently transplanted, medium-sized, packed for shipment with plenty of wet moss and straw, taken out of packings as soon as practicable and heeled in or planted close together in a trench so as to protect tree roots, or if that is impracticable, placed in a cool shed or cellar." The holes dug to receive them were to be ample and filled with rich soil, without manure. Pruning was to be done only under the special direction of the inspector.

Most of Robert's journal notes for the remainder of 1891 concern milk production and staff wages. He then had eleven cows milking. Six men worked the farm under Chester Ramsay, the head man; four men tended the grounds under Charles Halley, the stableman who also cared for the work, coach, and riding horses.

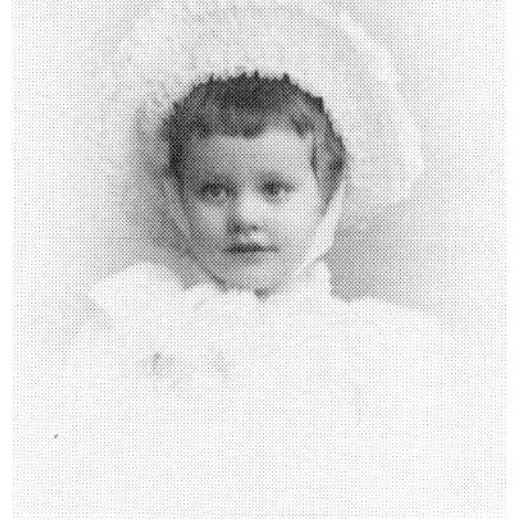

Margaret Lynch Suckley, "Daisy," age 1. Cabinet card by S. A. Thomas Studio, New York.

The year 1891 came to a close with a special glory. On December 20, Bessie presented Robert with their first daughter. Named Margaret Lynch after her Montgomery grandmother, she was beautiful, and even more important, weighed a healthy eight pounds. She would be called Daisy.

Throughout the 1892 and 1893 seasons, the Vauxes continued to supervise laying out the roads and walks. (The stone crusher was in constant use.) When Robert bought a house in New York City—41 East 80th Street—Downing was called in to work on that, too, both as architect and landscape architect. The correspondence between the two men became an exchange between friends. Robert lent Downing his transit and tripod, which Downing said enabled him "to do the most accurate work yet accomplished by me." When, on September 3, 1893, Bessie was safely delivered of twin girls, Katharine and Elizabeth, Robert included the good news in a business letter. Katharine's great-grandmother was Catherine and her grandmother Catharine. The family would spell her name in every way imaginable. The "K" and "a" were currently fashionable, and that is what Katharine herself adopted.)

However, the attic bedrooms still did not go forward. Vaux was anxious

Opposite: (left to right) Robin, age 4; Henry, age 7; and Arthur displaying the armour given to him on his seventh birthday. The helmet and breastplate were preserved, among many other toys, in Wilderstein's capacious attic. Cabinet cards by Rockwood Studio for Robin and Arthur; by S. A. Thomas Studio for Henry.

Left: Daisy, the guardian of her twin sisters, Katharine and Betty, 1895. Photograph by Rockwood Studio.

for the commission, but Robert kept putting him off. Vaux and Company were, in part, responsible for the delay. Radford had gone home to England for a visit, and, while there, decided to retire. Calvert Vaux was far less active than he had been. Downing, meanwhile, was dealing with an "embarrassment" arising from their work at the Niagara State Reservation; while excavating for the inclined railroad, their workmen had broken a city sewer line.

Far more critical, however, was the Panic of 1893. The most severe economic crisis the country had ever suffered, it began with deflation and the collapse of the stock market. In 1892, the Pennsylvania Railroad and four thousand banks failed. By 1893, currency was at a premium in New York. Unemployment was widespread. The returns on Robert's securities fell. (A significant percentage of them were tied to railroads.) He had great difficulty renting or selling his real estate.

Still, the panic did not immediately restrict the Suckleys' social life. They spent the winters in their New York town house, where the servants were presided over by a butler. Robert resigned from the Lawyers' Club. He hardly had time for it, for he was a member of the Players, Choral, City,

Racquet, Suburban Riding and Driving, and Metropolitan Clubs, as well as the Central Park Casino and Wood's gymnasium. Bessie joined the Colonial Dames and he the Society of Colonial Wars. They attended the opera, concerts, and theater. They were members of the New-York Society Library and the New-York Historical Society. Robert took Nummie and Robin to baseball games. With his men friends he played pinochle, pool, poker, and billiards. He was careful to keep up his subscription to the New York Social Register.

At Wilderstein Robert supervised the farm and gardens. At some point he started breeding fine horses. He became an avid cyclist, riding point to point on his Columbia bicycle. In one year, he recorded over two thousand miles, many of them accompanied by Nummie. He joined the Staatsburg Golf Club and, with Lynch Montgomery, became a dedicated, if not expert golfer. He grew prize chrysanthemums in his greenhouse and proudly exhibited them at the Annandale Flower Show. Although a vestryman and benefactor of the Episcopal Church of the Messiah, he continued the family tradition of support to local Methodist churches in myriad ways. In winter, he waited impatiently for the river to freeze so that he could sail his iceboats with fellow members of the Hudson River Ice-Yachting Club. He and Bessie continued to call on neighbors and to invite them to Wilderstein. Their circle of like-minded, socially correct acquaintances steadily increased.

In 1895, Robert indulged himself in another flurry of building. With the aid of his most versatile employee, William Wright, he added the office Vaux had designed and had a removable cold weather vestibule made for the front entrance. He extended the small bathroom serving his bedroom, by adding a marvel of cantilevered construction. He also bought a large, two-year-old conservatory from relatives in Flushing, Long Island. He may have intended to attach it to the space off the dining room where Tiffany had pleaded for a conservatory and where he had thought of placing a billiard room. There is no record, however, that he attempted to put it up. Rather, in June, he temporarily installed a billiard table he probably bought as a forty-first birthday present for himself, in the white and gold salon.

The children flourished. On Thanksgiving Day 1896, Suckley noted in his journal that all except the twins joined him and Bessie for dinner and that their behavior was excellent. They visited with their neighbors and their Bowne and Montgomery relatives almost daily. Aunts and cousins came to stay. It was a special pleasure when Grace Sands Hunt and Harry Montgomery, Bessie's older brother, were married after a long and dramatic courtship.

Wilderstein seemed to be fulfilling its promise in every way. However, Suckley's financial position did not improve. The panic had made serious inroads on his income. It was a strain to pay the house servants and farm workers. In January of 1897, before the spring planting, he decided that the most prudent solution was to reside for a time on the Continent. In a flurry of activity, he sold his livestock, reduced his employees to a bare-bones maintenance staff presided over by William Wright, and engaged multiple staterooms on the transatlantic liner *Westerland.*

On April 28, the Suckleys and two nursemaids sailed for Europe. Their destination was Switzerland, where they intended to spend two years. With various modifications, the family would reside abroad for the next decade.

Henry Eglinton Suckley, age 3, toddling across the south verandah. For most of his life Henry was called Nummie by his family. Snapshot taken by his father, summer 1890, using a hand-held Kodak camera of the kind introduced by George Eastman in 1888.

Robert, racing at Chateau d'Oex, Switzerland, with an unidentified woman, perhaps the female member of the local luge team, c. 1908.

A European Interlude

1897
1907

After a crossing marked by rolling seas, the *Westerland* arrived at Antwerp on May 8, 1897. Ten days later the Suckleys—increased by Bessie's sisters Nettie and Addie and her brother Harry and his wife Grace—had made their way to Geneva, the largest and richest city in Switzerland. French in tone, Protestant in religion, Swiss in orderliness and beautifully situated on an immense blue lake, it was, as Robert and Bessie knew from a visit during their extended wedding trip, a fashionable, gay place to be.

For a month they tarried, patronizing the fine shops and enjoying concerts in the Jardin des Anglais. They mingled with Americans of the "right sort," including Sara and James Roosevelt and Laura Astor Delano, their neighbors along the Hudson River. Nevertheless, as the weather warmed, Robert, for whom Switzerland's main attraction was its mountains, began looking for a summer retreat at a higher elevation. It was so near the peak season that resorts of first choice were already booked, but finally Pension Rosat in the village of Chateau d'Oex, a five-hour journey into the lower Alps, telegraphed they could have rooms commencing the first of July.

Located at an elevation of three thousand feet on the southern flank of Mt. Cray, Chateau d'Oex had long been noted as a center for outdoor sports—tennis, walking, and mountain climbing in the summer season; skiing, luging, and rink skating in the wintertime. Another attraction was the energizing and curative properties of the sweet, dry air. In 1897, there were sixteen hotels and pensions. The Grand Hotel, the largest, boasted one hundred rooms. The Rosat Pension and two others possessed sixty. None, the resort brochure emphasized, were sanitariums for consumptives.

Mme. Rosat, the proprietress, welcomed the Suckley contingent by hanging an American flag from the windows of their quarters in honor of the Fourth of July. The family settled in quickly, making friends with other

Pension Rosat, Chateau d'Oex, Switzerland. Home to the Suckleys from 1897-1907, and later, to Robert during his extended annual visits.

guests at the great dining tables and at teas, concerts, charades, and dances. Women gossiped in the parlors, while the men took full advantage of the billiard and smoking rooms. Out of doors, they made up walking and picnicking parties.

Robert and Harry played tennis on the first-rate courts of the Chateau d'Oex tennis club and arranged lessons for the boys. Often, on their bicycling and easier climbing expeditions, they took Nummie and Robin along. Arthur and the girls, lumped together as "the children," were minded by the two nursemaids and, in spare moments, by Bessie and her sisters. It was a virtually carefree summer. Loathe to leave, they stayed on through the autumn. The days remained much the same, except that Harry went home and the nursemaid, Marie, metamorphosed into a governess. Bessie and Robert put on a party for the children at the Rosat for Daisy's sixth birthday. A guest named Mr. White provided a tree for the Christmas festivities. A Lady Walsham and other ladies managed a sugarplum and small present giving event. The Suckleys were fast making Pension Rosat their home.

Snow brought adepts of winter sports to Chateau d'Oex. Robert became a devotee of luging. (The configuration of a luge was then somewhere between that of a toboggan and a bobsled.) Women, as well as men, enjoyed the sport both for pleasure and the excitement of competitive racing. Occasionally, even Bessie was persuaded to join in. On fine moonlit evenings, skating took precedence over dancing in the salon.

Still, Robert kept in close touch with his affairs in America. He corresponded by letter with William Wright whom he had left in charge of Wilderstein. With Harry, who was trading his securities and overseeing the management of his real estate, his preferred medium of communication was cablegram, employing an elaborate code they had jointly devised. It was a successful system. Robert's securities account showed a nice increase.

Pleased, he decided the family should remain at Chateau d'Oex for an indefinite period of time. It would be necessary for him, however, to return to the United States for a month or so to check up on Wilderstein and his investments. As always with Harry, business and pleasure merged. The highlights in the latter category seem to have been evening excursions to the Pleasure Palace and to the Wild West Show. Flying trips to Rhinebeck found all secure at Wilderstein in the loyal hands of Wright.

Back at Rosat by the end of March 1898, Robert went on long walking trips with Henri Alioth, a Swiss who would become his closest European friend. He also took up golf again. He found a male tutor for Nummie. "The children," this time including Robin, remained under the tutelage of a governess. Robin undoubtedly spoke for Arthur and quite possibly for his sisters, too, when he wrote: "A new governess is coming here to teach us. We are not looking forward to her arrival at all, for, perhaps you know that we hate lessons and governesses."

The summer of 1898 at Chateau d'Oex. Bessie with the children and the nursemaid Marie. Daisy holding a kitten, Arthur a tennis racket, and Marie a puppy.

As the year wore on the family became increasingly divided into two distinct groups. Robin was now grown-up enough sometimes to join his father and Nummie in outdoor activities. They walked, skied, biked, and climbed together. As the boys grew more proficient in tennis, Robert would occasionally hit a ball with them. Both boys were encouraged to take up the violin. Robert as well as the boys took lessons. Robert also shared his *Engineering Magazine* with them, and subscribed to *Boy's Own Companion* for them.

In the fall of 1899, it became evident that Nummie, now twelve years old, needed a more formal education than a local tutor could provide. Robert chose a small boarding school called La Villa in Ouchy, Lausanne, two and a half hours distant by train. Bessie approved only because careful attention was given to each student's physical well-being as well as to his academic work.

At the same time, perhaps as a reward for suffering the governess, Robert took Robin with him when he went to the United States for a month's stay. Bessie was not happy about this break in the family circle. There was, however, not much she could do. A little note from Robin, jubilantly stating, "I am now seated in Uncle Harry's office," and a letter from Robert, telling her he had taken him to the automobile show in Boston, were of little comfort to her. Moreover, when they got back to Rosat, Robert saw no reason why Robin should not join Nummie at La Villa. That left Arthur and the girls to be hovered over by Bessie, Addie, and their governess at Rosat. The children's chief joy was a little dog named Scamp in which

The winter of 1898 at Chateau d'Oex. Robin, Arthur, Daisy, Betty and Katharine.

Robert had given each of them a tradable one-sixth interest.

The Suckleys did not treat the advent of the twentieth century with any special celebration. They seem simply to have slipped into it. Nummie, typical of most boys new to boarding school, complained that La Villa was boring and told his mother to send him American stamps with long pictures on them, the game of "Flugo of the White Squadron," and suspenders "as my pants are always coming down." She added a rich plum cake, too. Betty contracted diphtheria, so often a killing disease, but she was such a strong and buoyant little person, there never seems to have been any question of her recovery.

Summertime brought more tennis. Nummie won the men's singles tournament. Violin lessons continued, and Arthur began piano lessons. All the children took drawing lessons. In August, Robert treated Bessie and Addie to a music lover's excursion to Oberammergau and Munich, where they enjoyed Wagner's *Tristan and Isolde* and *Lohengrin* as well as traditional Tyrolean music.

When the fall term came around, Robert dropped Robin off at La Villa, then took Nummie on a week's jaunt to the Paris Exposition. Back at LaVilla, Nummie became an avid soccer as well as tennis player. (He wrote demanding six tennis balls, the six being underlined seven times.) He was satisfied with his marks, too. But he was not pleased with the daily massage and the breakfast porridge his mother had ordered. Robin's main concern was that the Kiddy, as he called Arthur, not use his bicycle. "It will fall every few minutes," he complained, "and the Kiddy would never think of dirtying his hands with cleaning the wheels or anything of that sort." Soon he had a more serious worry. He did not know where his mother was. "Please tell me where mama lives," he wrote his father, "because I cannot write to her otherwise."

The unsettling fact was that in early December 1900, Robert took Bessie, at her request, to the Quisana sanitarium in Baden-Baden, Germany. Her stated hope was to find a cure for chronic indigestion, but in reality, she was suffering a nervous breakdown. Robert must have been forewarned. The letters she wrote to him while he was in the United States veer suddenly from abject pleading for his sympathy to authoritarian outbursts criticizing his physical appearance. On the eve of their fifteenth wedding anniversary she flagellated herself for not being clever or healthy enough to supply his needs, then berated him for allowing "his splendid youth to disappear in wreaths of smoke, nothing but the perfume left behind where there was so much talent and power."

Robin, Henry and Arthur, 1903. Robin and Arthur, cartes de visite by Frèd Boissonnas, Geneva. Cabinet card of Henry by Lacroix fils et Rogeat, Geneva.

The immediate cause of her collapse was probably her feeling of abandonment when first Nummie, then Robin left the nest. But obviously, her marriage had not been a happy one. On both sides, many of the complaints were classic. Bessie scolded because, when at home, Robert retired to his pipe, his papers, and the company of his men friends and, when away, he wrote only the occasional post card, rarely a letter. In turn, he upbraided her for being unaffectionate and inept at running their household or managing their children. Their life expectations and needs simply did not mesh. She had always preferred the social excitement of the city; he increasingly enjoyed the multiple challenges of the country. Physical sport was necessary to him. Even after her years of childbearing ceased, Bessie avoided strenuous exercise. He was an ardent amateur musician; she had no talent for playing. Moreover, despite their many children, all evidence points to their being sexually incompatible. There was no connecting door between their separate bedrooms at Wilderstein; it was necessary to go into the public hall to get from one to the other. Her seven full-term pregnancies and several miscarriages in less than ten years had left her not only exhausted, but dispirited. It is highly probable her physical and mental state was another reason they had left Wilderstein for Switzerland. Robert's recent anniversary present to Bessie was a handsome brooch in the form of a spider.

Just how deep-rooted Bessie's malady was would soon become evident. It took the form of frenzied and sometimes ferocious anxiety about her children's health, especially that of her boys. Decades later, when Daisy was going through the family correspondence, she wrote on the margin of one of these letters: "A bad time with Robin & Arthur delicate. Elizabeth herself, run down."

The sudden absence of their mother was devastating to the four youngest children living at Rosat. Arthur was ten years old, Daisy not quite nine and the twins just seven. Under the guidance of Marie they wrote loving little get-well notes, illustrated with pencil drawings of their pets and escapades and themselves. From LaVilla Robin wrote plaintively to his father, "Are the kiddy and the children M'rie and Scamp all right." The week before Christmas he was desperate to learn what their vacation plans might be. Nummie simply clammed up.

Robert's partial solution was to send Arthur to La Villa, where Bessie saw to it he was placed in special care. Made to lie down for an hour before dinner and an hour afterwards, he complained he had no time for lessons. He was not even permitted to go outside. There was a glimmer of hope that family life might improve when Bessie transferred herself to a sanitarium on the outskirts of Montreux. However, the reason she gave for the change was that the doctor at Baden-Baden refused her sleeping draughts, told her that hypnotism would do her no good, and was, in short, "all business, no sympathy." What soon became evident is that she wished to be within easier reach of Robert and her children, more to control than to nurture them.

"Gorgeous, expensive and very quiet" according to Bessie, the new sanitarium, LaColline, followed the method devised by the renowned Philadelphia psychiatrist S. Weir Mitchell to cure what were then known as female aneurysms, that is, any departure from the accepted standard of sweetness, calm, and grace with which "true women" were thought to be naturally endowed. It called for complete bed rest: no reading, no writing, no drawing, no communication with friends. Only selected family—usually the father or husband—were allowed as visitors, and sometimes not even they. In addition, the patient was stuffed with bland food. During the initial stage, the cure depended on mental and sensory deprivation to achieve the patient's total submission to the doctor. The cure was known to result in madness, but that was blamed on the patient's lack of docility.

Bessie, however, was far from docile. Almost as soon as she arrived at LaColline, she plucked Robin out of school and brought him to the sanitarium where he was confined to bed to cure supposed digestive problems. "Why did Robin have to go to LaColline. He was very upset by it," Nummie wrote angrily to his father. In response, Bessie sent orders to La Villa that Nummie was to be dosed with cod liver oil and milk after every meal. The hated porridge for breakfast was still an order, too. Nummie was so disgusted—and probably so terrified—that he told his father he had decided not to go to Rosat, but to remain at Ouchy for the Easter holidays.

In June, Robert took Arthur and the girls on a most satisfactory excursion to Heinrichbad, an ancient and picturesque town in German Switzerland. Its main attraction for the children, other than having their father with them, was a park called Paradis that featured live monkeys. Robin continued at LaColline until somehow, in July, he managed to extricate himself. On August 29, Robert noted in his diary with due pride that Robin had won the singles in the Chateau d'Oex tennis tournament. By then Nummie had taken his place with Bessie at LaColline, as a companion, however, rather than an invalid. He was angry and utterly bored.

For the next three years, this pattern persisted in varying, though frighteningly similar forms. The boys were placed in a succession of schools and sanitariums, usually escaping to Rosat in the summer. The girls remained at Rosat, cared for by Marie and, when he was not engaged in mountain sports with his men friends or vacationing in the United States, by their father. They were taught by governesses, mainly Mademoiselle Blum, for whom Daisy, especially, developed a strong respect..

In 1902, Nummie, now fifteen years old, was packed off to Basel where he was taught by private tutors and required to eat porridge between meals and before he went to bed. Robin and Arthur started off as a pair at La Villa. They got along very well, playing soccer, tennis, ping pong, and cards for recreation. Arthur bought a fine little steam engine, which he paid for by

Robin, Arthur, and Henry with their father (far right) and members of the Chateau d'Oex tennis club. All the boys would become excellent players.

selling a five dollar American stamp at a satisfying markup. Robin concocted an ingenious chemical-based lighting device so that he could read at night. Then, Bessie whisked the two off to the Clinique Generale de Florissant in Geneva where she and they, she believed, would be at last made well. Arthur was required to swallow a pipe every night "to draw off the gas" and was subjected to a cold shower every morning. A great, quiet nurse of whom he was terrified made him eat cream-based soups and drink milk for nourishment. Robin's treatment was again complete bed rest. Bessie bought him a little canary to allay the tedium. "If he tires of it," she wrote Robert, "I can give it to Daisy for Christmas. Unfortunately he has not yet developed the voice the man assured me he would have." When Robin was at last allowed to attend school, he found he liked geometry, math, and history. He tried hard to get a medal in one of them. "You see I have never had a prize before, excepting in tennis," he explained to his father. Bessie herself repeated the calming cure, with her own variations. The doctor would not allow her to walk, so she hired a carriage to take her on pleasant excursions about town. Still she could not sleep, even after several doses of valerian.

Mademoiselle Blum, the Suckley girls' Swiss tutor.

The next year, Nummie was enrolled in a school in Kroningfeld, Germany to prepare him for a good German high school or an American boarding school. Bessie took Arthur and Robin to St. Moritz to try still another cure. She underwent electric shock treatments—and suddenly she was drinking tea, dancing, and shopping at the various spas. Not needing the boys quite so urgently, she enrolled Robin in a nearby English school designed for floating internationals and sent Arthur to the Diakonessenhaus in Heidelberg, where his health was daily monitored by a nurse.

Somehow, the boys survived this fractured life, Nummie by learning how to distance himself from the family and Robin and Arthur by catching hold of whatever came to hand. Their father did not overtly sympathize with them, at least in writing. In fact, he seldom visited them. Perhaps, his behavior was caused by memories of his sister's slow decline and the horror of his own Rutsen's sudden death. Still, few families in those days escaped similar and worse tragedies. It was not uncommon for diphtheria or pneumonia or scarlet fever to take one child after another. The fact remains that Robert did not take strong action to give his boys continuity of education or to prevent Bessie from subjecting them to excessive medical and psychological treatment. He did, however, send them bicycles and Kodak cameras and magazine subscriptions. And he saw to it that they continued their music lessons. Robin became an excellent amateur violinist and Arthur played the piano very well and the flute moderately well. As far as Robin's and Arthur's delicate health was concerned, their trials were far from over, but it is good to note Robin would live to be a wiry eighty-five-year-old and Arthur was still capable of playing clever tennis the year before he died at age eighty-five. But, Bessie would outlive Robert by nearly thirty-three years, and would never cease to mold their lives.

While the boys were involved in this game of changing schools and sanitariums, the girls led an unremarkable life at Rosat. They made friends among the few children who lived there and delighted in the company of their father when he offered it. The focus of Robert's life in Switzerland was sport, which often took him away from Rosat. When there, he played billiards and cards and smoked cigars and imbibed whatever alcoholic beverage was popular with his men friends. All the hotels of Chateau d'Oex offered a perpetual round of entertainments. Robert was not entirely neglectful for, in that era, fathers were not expected to be intimately involved with raising children, especially daughters. Parents of their social class generally left the day-to-day work to servants, governesses and tutors. Certainly, he was proud of his daughters' accomplishments. When Daisy won first prize in a piano recital he was thrilled. When she won second prize and a purse of money in a midget class luging contest, he rewarded her with an extra two dollars. He was equally pleased that all three girls succeeded in a challenging climb. He was delighted, too, when they appeared in pretty dresses.

In reality, Robert's life was not as satisfactory or as self-indulgent as on the surface it might have seemed. He struggled to keep his weight down and he suffered increasingly from gout. He constantly worried about the cost of the sanitariums, spas, hotels, schools, and fashionable dressmakers. As

Robert's favorite pastimes in Switzerland were skiing, luging and mountain climbing. Some of his excursions into the mountains were dangerous. Others were larks, punctuated with bread, cheese, wine and a restorative smoke. Inscribed by Robert on the reverse:"Dobbs and his house, Hill and his dog, Beauclerk and his cigarette." August 1905.

Robert showing off his Orient 2-cylinder automobile to Grace Hunt Montgomery at Wildercliff, 1904.

for his role as a husband, he became resigned to its absence. Bessie had not given up her convoluted verbal outbursts, deliberately aimed at wounding him: "I am always wishing you would prefer our society to that of those idle men." As for the children, the most positive thing they learned from this painfully fragmented upbringing was the importance of befriending each other whenever and as well as they could.

In the spring of 1904, Robert made his usual trip back to the United States. No sooner had he arrived in New York than he took an action that would transform all of their lives. He bought an Orient Buckboard automobile—"$425, lamp and horn brought it up to $433 which HEM [Harry] paid for me." Immediately, he shipped it via the Saugerties night boat to Wilderstein. Accompanying it was a chauffeur who would stay long enough to teach Wright how to run and care for it. "HEM's 2 horses & the automobile arrived about 7 a.m.," he joyfully recorded. "The automobile very well. Harry went to Homestead in it. Returned via Village and Rhinecliff in 25 minutes. I took a ride around through the Morton place."

Enthralled by the recreational possibilities of motorized travel, he next bought a Columbia motor bicycle through Smillie & Co. of Rhinebeck, which cost somewhere in the neighborhood of three hundred dollars, horn and lamp added. The rest of his visit he spent touring around, calling on relatives and friends, carefully noting his times in his journal. His best run from the Wildercliff farm barn to Main Street in Poughkeepsie was fifty-two minutes. When he returned to Europe, he carried it with him as baggage. Writing his "dearest Bessie," advising her of his arrival at Geneva the morning of May 24th, he told her, "I will look you all up and spend that day only as I must push on to Chateau d'Oex to get out summer clothes," by which he meant he would ride around the mountain roads on his Columbia.

Maiden voyage of Columbia motorbicycle outfitted with passenger trailer. Henry driving, his father in the trailer. Petites Dalles, France, 1904.

Robert seldom missed a day of biking except when it was in the shop for repairs or it had been preempted by Robin, who was, if anything a more enthusiastic rider. On Robin's first excursion, he collided with the son of the local chemist who was ambling along on his bicycle. The boy's bicycle was badly damaged (Robert would make reparations) but Robert proudly noted, "Robin was only bruised and rode the machine back, 2 spokes broken."

Both because Bessie's doctors had been touting the therapeutic value of a sojourn by the sea, and because his climbing companion Aloith would be visiting there, Robert rented a house in the artists' colony of Petites Dalles, Boulogne-sur-Mer, Normandy, France, that summer. His plan was to stay six weeks, then take Nummie to Phillips Exeter Academy. Laden with eighteen pieces of luggage, the motorbike, bicycles, tennis rackets, and a cook from Geneva, the entire family, including Marie, arrived at the resort in mid-July. They bathed in the sea, played tennis on Alioth's cousin's court, motorbiked, and went for drives in a rented chauffeured automobile. The motorbike, for which Robert bought a trailer, was in constant motion. Even when the Geneva cook and the maid decamped (Alioth supplied substitutes), it was a relaxing existence. The only excitement occurred when the Casino and the villa adjoining it burned down in the middle of the night. Robert, Nummie and Robin helped pass the fire buckets.

At the end of August, Robert and Nummie—for the moment referred to by his father as Montgomery—departed for the United States. Their farewell procession to the railway station was magnificent indeed. Alioth and Robert left Petites Dalles first in a wagon carting two trunks. Montgomery and Robin followed riding the motorbike and trailer. The rest of the family piled into the rented automobile. It was a poignant *rite de passage* for both father and son. To mark the event Robert had bought a beautiful

Vaucheron watch in a gunmetal case which he would present to Montgomery when they were at last alone aboard ship.

Nummie, who had been parted from his relatives and Wilderstein since he was ten years old, was ecstatic to be back home. He and his father took meals at Wildercliff—it had been rented to Harry in exchange for repairs—and visited the Eugene Lynches who had built "an awfully nice house" named Mansakenning three miles southeast of the village. They also dined at Glenburn. "The house has changed awfully and is not nearly so pretty outwardly as before. It is nevertheless very comfortable," Nummie wrote his mother. They rented a late model motorcycle from Smillie's that went twice as fast as their Columbia. After Robert delivered Nummie to Exeter, he spent most of his time in America driving, improving, and fixing the Orient. The holiday was too short.

When he returned to Switzerland, Robert found the depressing patterns of the past had not changed. He was pleased, however, that from his new school in Geneva Robin mirrored his enthusiasm for motor transport. "How does the machine work?" he demanded, referring to the motorcycle. "How do the accumulators perform their part? Does the trailer go all right? and have you put in the springs yet? You can buy a shop-soiled FN [France Nationale] motorcycle down here for about 650 francs. Why do you not get it." Robert resisted the impulse. Instead he bought his friend Dobbs' FN.

The news from Exeter was good, too. It was as if Nummie, having had seven lean years, was about to enjoy seven fat. "We have a great deal of freedom compared to my other schools," he wrote, "and I expect I shall like it very much." He spent the Thanksgiving weekend in Boston with "a few fellows," an excursion into society that prompted the brotherly comment, "Are the twins and Daisy taking dancing lessons? They ought to. I wish there was a dancing school here and I would join it."

During Christmas vacation, Nummie stayed with his Uncle Harry. He

At the railroad station. (left to right) Unidentified, twin, Daisy, unidentified, twin, Marie, unidentified, Robert, Bessie, and Robin, 1904.

went to the theater almost every night, met all the family in Flushing, and got in a couple of days ice-boating in Rhinebeck. Back at Exeter, he joined a fraternity and went to two dances. Describing all this social activity to his mother he teasingly concluded, "And I suppose you will be making your spring trip down to Geneva to get your summer outfit and trousseau." Bessie had, indeed, taken up residence in that cosmopolitan city.

Daisy, now thirteen, became a substitute mother at Rosat, tending both Robin, who was feeling poorly, and her father, who was inflicted with gout and toothache. "I hope you are continuing to improve as we all need you very much here," she wrote her mother in what can only be described as a stern letter. "I hope you will not stay two months as you say Arthur has to stay that time. I am very much afraid you will. Have you had a letter from Nummie yet? I hope you have as I do not want you to be anxious about him. But you must really not be so about Robin as he is perfectly well and takes his gruel regularly. He has an egg every morning or milk toast. Papa is much better." To back up their self-sufficiency, Robert wrote Bessie, Robin "takes great interest in his music both violin and piano. He goes out on the motorcycle. Thinks nothing of running down to Bulle & back in 2½ hours. Daisy and the twins have been getting a lot of beautiful dresses with balloon sleeves. Tres chic!"

Arthur, still at the Clinique, was not so fortunate. His regime was "swallowing a pipe and two applications of oil etc. every morning." Virtually

Advertisement for the France Nationale motorcycle Robert bought second hand in 1905 with Robin's notations. The "FN" would become Robin's proud possession. Just before his death in 1974, he gave it to a friend. Then in poor condition, it since has been restored.

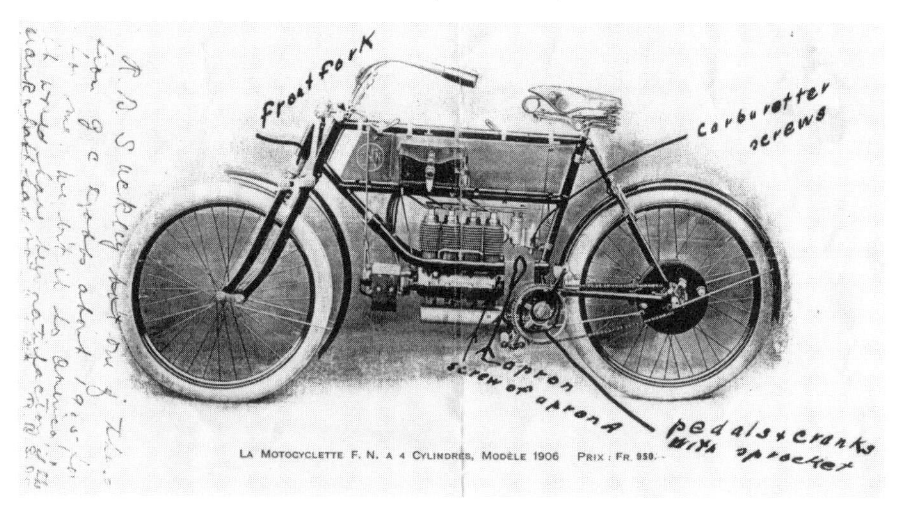

imprisoned, he had become the desired "patient patient." Bessie herself was being treated for anemia and was wearing a tight elastic below her waist to mitigate a possible prolapsed womb. Since the latter condition was not difficult to diagnose, that statement to Robert may well have been intended as a reproach for her multiple pregnancies. Moreover, she could not resist admonishing him about his puffy eyes and lackluster expression which she found so unattractive.

It was not until the middle of April 1905 that Robert escaped to New York. In a letter to Bessie full of enticing gossip, he wrote, "Nummie is a perfect giant and looks extremely well. I think he must be six feet now.... Glenburn is having a constant succession of visitors most of whom (if not all) arrive in auto, yacht or private car. The HEM's are living for the moment in three houses. Parents in N.Y., children at the Homestead & work men at Wildercliff." Nettie and Addie were in residence at the Lynches' handsome Mansakenning and were "blooming." Alice Olin and her husband Tracy Dows were negotiating for the Langdon Place at Hyde Park. Jack Astor, who was becoming a friend, had given him a tour of Ferncliff. The Mortons bought a donkey from him for their three-year-old grandchild. Finally, he had enrolled Robin at Exeter. That clinched it for Bessie. She told Robert that she, not he, would accompany Robin and Nummie to Exeter in the fall.

When Bessie and the two boys docked at New York in September, Harry, Alan, and Addie were there to take them to Rhinebeck, where they would stay at Wildercliff while she summoned strength to put Wilderstein in proper living order. Bessie could not have been happier. Her first letter to Robert proclaims a transformation in mood and style that would have as great an impact on her family as had her nervous collapse in 1901:

> Such a surprise, when the automobile with the two boys and chauffeur drove up to the door yesterday. I was quite stupefied and cannot realize that we have such a thing, yet we put on our coats at once when it came and drove to Mansakenning where I had an enthusiastic welcome. The machine is a perfect beauty, just the size I would have chosen, not too large and cumbersome but medium size and so handsome. It is simply perfect. Harry, Addie, the two boys and myself got into it very comfortably, also the chauffeur. We had a lovely time.

In late September she accompanied the boys to Exeter. Despite Nummie's plea that they take a suite in Peabody Hall instead of Dunbar, which he said housed all the school toughs on probation, Bessie had remained firm, choosing to forget that Robin was seventeen and Nummie eighteen years old.

> How delighted we were with Dunbar Hall. If Robin is strong enough he will do well. The food at Dunbar is excellent & Mrs. Clarke a strong kindly motherly woman, but of course no individual care is given of the boys unless they get ill. There is no one to remind them to put on their rubbers, to have their shoes mended, to put on an overcoat & the numerous little things a mother would see to. All depends on the boy himself & for this reason I doubt if Robin can live without some care of this kind. It is a fearful wrench (& I do not exaggerate) to leave him, and I cannot bear to leave him thinking of all that might so easily happen to him. The doctor is to send me a postal each week that I am here and knowing his condition I hope will be guided in doing what is best for him. He is so anxious to take an interest in everything & always over tiring himself. He must not put a strain on his heart. His pulse is beating at 95 to 100 instead of 70 to 75 as it should be.

In addition, she warned Robert not to give the boys too much money. She had noticed Robin's gambling aboard ship. Robert agreed with the need to keep them on a short rein. Robin solved his financial problem neatly. He joined the orchestra and, when he played for dancing, got two dollars a night.

As soon as she got back to Wilderstein, Bessie set to work putting the house in order with the will of a seasoned housekeeper. "I have been sorting out our linen & handsome china & will put all away in a locked closet," she wrote Robert. She examined the furniture for moths and had a cleaning woman put out roach salt and fumigate the closets. "I have never seen the place look so pretty," She added. "The grass looks so green & fresh. The dear little calf is always on the lawn tied in different places."

She was delighted too that all the new friends Robert had made among the "river people," as well as the old connections he had revived, welcomed

Snapshot of Henry and Robin on vacation in Switzerland, August 24, 1905. The girls have not been identified.

her, begging her to visit and take meals with them. The Crosbys, Chanlers, and Delanos came to call. So did Mrs. Morton, who was anxious to know when the boys would be at Wilderstein. (The Mortons had five daughters.) Margaret Chanler invited the family to the fiftieth anniversary of the Red Hook Episcopal Church. But of all the new acquaintances, Mrs. Ernest Crosby fascinated her most. Her Grasmere, a lovely added-onto Federal house, was quite the gayest place on the river. Then, too, her son Maunsell was at Harvard and Nummie's age.

Henry ready for a tennis match.

Even the gossip revolving around the Astors entertained Bessie. Jack Astor, she wrote Robert, was rumored to have had several women at Newport, one a mulatto, and he was also making advances to the Duchess of Malborough, then a guest at Ferncliff. (The fast life at Ferncliff was undoubtedly one of the inspirations for novelist Edith Wharton's just-completed *The House of Mirth*. Astor and his high-flying wife, Philadelphia blue-blood Ava Willing, had long been living as strangers under the same roof.) Bessie's only criticism was that a man of such loose morals was allowed to serve as a warden of the local Episcopal church.

Meanwhile, back in Switzerland Daisy and the twins had been sent to a boarding school at Heinrichbad, where learning how to run a household went hand in hand with earning an academic degree. Although Daisy was almost fifteen and the twins were twelve, this was their first experience with institutional education. Daisy was happy there. "I have one great piece of news to tell you. It is that I have bought a dear little bird," she wrote her mother and, in an ingratiating bit of flattery, asked her to name it. By the middle of October she had two birds. The new one ate out of her hand and she let him fly about the room. She also made friends with a little colt named Horza, who came when called and never bit or kicked. This called forth all her memories of Wilderstein: "I am just *longing* to be at Wilderstein now! It must be so lovely keeping house with Aunt Addie. Have you seen my donkey yet? (I call the one we always used to use with the donkey-cart mine." Returning to reality, she told her mother she was foolish to worry about them. Her proof was that she weighed 104 pounds.

With the girls, who were never her primary targets anyway, cared for by their school, only the long suffering Arthur was within Bessie's grasp. He had spent a dreadful spring at LaColline, deprived of all diversions, even flute and piano playing. All the doctor would say was that Arthur must lead an ordered life and eat simple foods until he became older and stronger. For once, Arthur revolted. "Wasn't that exactly what I said before and can't I get simple food and lead a regular life out of this *sanitarium*," he exploded in an angry, sarcastic letter to his mother. "Do you not think that I am repaid for all the annoyance that I have had this spring by the knowledge that I must lead a regular life and eat simple food. I wish you could come here some time to talk things over. I am very anxious to get down to Geneva & begin lessons with Dufour," a first-rate violin teacher. He then lashed out at Caper, a combined tutor, companion, and male nurse whom Bessie had engaged to watch over him and who spoiled even his going to church, the only occasion he had for seeing anyone he knew. Reminding his mother that she had failed to return his watch, Arthur wound up this bitter letter, "I suppose your delight at reaching Geneva made you forget all about it."

The result was that Arthur was sent, with Caper, to a sanitarium at Gland, near Geneva. Daisy, who had inspected the place beforehand, described the countryside as very quiet, the rooms as nice, and the doctor attentive. It was not long before Bessie received word that, in the doctor's opinion, there was nothing much the matter with Arthur. When Robert got this good news, he promptly enrolled Arthur in Exeter.

In the middle of August 1906, Nummie sailed to America by himself. At the end of that month, Bessie, Robin, and Arthur met up with Robert, who had been enjoying a little sojourn with Aloith and Dobbs in Paris. The entire party proceeded to Le Havre where they settled Bessie in her cabin and exchanged last goodbyes with Arthur and Robin.

On arrival in New York, Bessie immediately took the boys to "Wilderstine," as Arthur then spelled it. His main interest was being driven around the countryside in the Orient by his Uncle Harry's chauffeur. On one run, they made Poughkeepsie in fifty-five minutes. He was equally pleased when Harry entertained him and his brothers in New York. Harry gave them lunch at the Stock Exchange and, afterwards, took them for a ride in his Stevens. Robin, who considered himself a car expert, admitted that although it was not so comfortable as the Orient, its motor was far superior. Displaying the gift for mechanics that had long been a mainstay, he explained to his father that the engine, composed of smooth cones, with none of the little projecting parts that caused so much trouble on the Orient, was very easy to clean. In fact, he advised him not to spend any more money on

The Suckley girls in elegant dresses. Photograph by Frèd Boissonnas, Geneva, 1906.

such a jerry-built machine than was absolutely necessary to keep it running.

While the boys were jaunting, Bessie put the house and grounds in order with the help of Nettie and Addie. "The place looks so pretty I love it better each time I see it," she bubbled over in a long 3 a.m. letter to Robert. She asked permission to have Wright prune the shrubs and small trees: they were hardy, but all of their strength seemed to be running into height. Bessie's expanding social circle also charmed her. All the "swells" were going to the dear Lynches' Mansakenning. The Dows, having abandoned the Langdon's Hyde Park property, were creating a vast estate with extensive roads, superintendent's house, farmers' cottages, and barns on riverview property contiguous to the Wildercliff farm and the Wilderstein power house. It would be called Fox Hollow. The Chapmans, too, had built a new house. Named Sylvania, it was on riverfront land adjoining Rokeby where as Elizabeth Chanler, Mrs. Chapman had grown up. Margaret Chanler of Rokeby was to be married to Richard Aldrich, a music critic. Forty-three, white haired, plain looking, and, though intelligent, a stutterer, he did not seem to Bessie nearly nice enough for Margaret. But the verandah of that venerable mansion was being decorated for the wedding by Margaret's brother, the fashionable muralist "Sheriff" Bob Chanler, and that caught Bessie's fancy.

In mid-September, with Addie for support, Bessie took Arthur and Robin to Exeter, where they each had nice rooms in the well-supervised Dunbar Hall. The problem Arthur had yet to face was that his catch-as-catch-can education had left him ill-prepared for a large, established, academically exacting, and to him, foreign, boys' boarding school where, in order to succeed, he must fit in. The odds were he would be the oldest boy in his class. Even worse, he spoke with an English accent, wore European-style clothes, and had acquired European mannerisms. Nummie and Robin had suffered similar disadvantages and seemed to be surmounting them, but they had been older when they went abroad to live and had not remained there so long. Nowhere near so cut off from normal schooling, they had enjoyed far more independence and had acquired more self-confidence. With Robin to guide him, Arthur made the best he could of Exeter. He joined the chess and checker club and waited impatiently for the school to finish its fourteen new tennis courts. Robin, who had joined the mandolin club and was playing second violin in the orchestra, encouraged him to take up the flute again.

After installing the boys at Exeter, Bessie and Addie went on to Cambridge where they spent a week, taking rooms on Buckingham Street within walking distance of Nummie's Harvard College dormitory, Claverly Hall. Bessie examined Claverly thoroughly. The building was very attractive inside and out, she wrote Robert, and she was pleased that each boy had a sitting room with a fireplace as well as a bed room and a private bath. However, she did not like the fact that Nummie's quarters were on the ground floor. There would be continual temptations for young fellows to drop in, and the windows were too close to the ground, she complained. Before Nummie arrived the following day, she was determined to exchange them for rooms on a higher floor. Bessie also examined Cambridge closely. The houses, she wrote Robert, were pretty and very neatly kept. Although it was a quiet, out-of-the-way place, there were lovely concerts, art exhibitions and lectures by the best men all winter. In a two-hour chauffeur ride arranged by Robin, she had seen that the road to Albany (i.e., the Hudson Valley) was so wide and smooth it was possible to drive a steady thirty miles per hour upon it. In short, she thought it the very place for them to spend their winters so that they would be near the boys and sometimes be with them. Fortunately, that particular dream never became a reality.

Yet, despite her yen for Cambridge, Bessie was extraordinarily content at Wilderstein. In her last letter before returning to Europe, Bessie wrote Robert: "This house looks so clean and lovely, I am more in love with the place than ever before. I enjoy my room so much and am writing here at my desk. Nettie and Addie are preparing for bed and have been sitting in the library beside a fire. The trees are a mass of green and red and though the sky has been overcast, one would think the sun was shining, the woods are so aglow with yellow leaves… The days fly by and if you and the little girls were here I should be so glad. I long to have them associated with it." He could not have been happier when he received it.

Meanwhile, Robert had placed the girls in the more academically challenging English school in Fribourg. To a striking extent for a conservative in those times, he wanted his daughters to have educational opportunities similar to those he was endeavoring to provide for his boys. Daisy studied diligently and practiced the piano an hour and a half a day. The twins teamed up in going along with the minimum they could get away with.

Back at Rosat, Robert played occasional bridge and poker in the evenings. His gout was so painful it curtailed his outdoor sports and his visits to Fribourg. After a dreary Christmas there with Bessie and the girls, he finally decided he could not live in a self-imposed limbo. The time had come to reunite the family permanently at Wilderstein.

Bessie was perfectly happy with that decision, except that while the boys were in school and college, she intended to spend winters in Cambridge. The very thought of his mother's hovering presence outraged Nummie and he told her so. "I hear that it is definitely decided," he wrote,

> that we are going to live away from home for another year in a place where we don't know a soul and where we will be cut off from everywhere and every body. I hardly see the necessity of your coming to Cambridge on my account as I have lived away at school since I was thirteen and ought to be able to take care of myself by this time. I should think in fact that we all ought to be able to get along without direct supervision. Arthur seems to be thriving away from home influences where he can eat and drink what he wants and go to bed when he feels like it. Of course, I should like to have you all here very much, but I think that it will break up my college life somewhat especially if I live with you. You know that you would not like me to have fellows in my room at all hours of the day and night making a lot of noise. I do not see why we cannot live at Rhinebeck for the greater part of the year and go to N.Y. for a few months in the winter. There must be some apartments which would be desirable as well as cheap. In our nomadic way of living the girls have not had a single opportu-

> nity of making friends who are ladies... I am sorry because Daisy will not have a chance to meet nice girls in New York, unless, of course, she goes to some school near there. Living in Cambridge would be very weary for everyone, especially papa who does not like the city.

Robert kept his own counsel on the subject of Cambridge. He was occupied with bidding farewell to their life in the Alps. He took the girls on a series of challenging ski expeditions. They dined on *truite au bleu* at Montbovan. When he and Dobbs climbed the Gummfluh, he invited Daisy to come along with them. In September, Daisy gave a goodbye tea for her friends in the sun room at Rosat. On October 6, Mme. Rosat put on a splendid dinner. On October 10, 1907, Robert wrote in his diary: "Cold meat tea chez Reuss. Much weeping at departure. All friends at station, 7 p.m. train. Lights moving up and down at the windows of Rosat as our train passed by." Succinct as the entry is, it is obvious that he was deeply moved. Just before leaving the pension, he had carefully selected a dozen chestnuts from the tree outside the Rosat dining room to plant on the grounds at Wilderstein.

Daisy cleverly adapted this postcard advertisement for Suchard chocolate to commemorate a thrilling expedition with her father and his friend Dobbs in the late summer of 1907. She inked in a full skirt to the figure she identified as herself and labeled it "Suckley IV." The message on the reverse, sent to her mothers, says: "This is a picture of when we were climbing the Gummfluh. I thought it better to put in the names as you might not recognize us. I hope you approve of my costume."

Mr. Dobbs.
Suckley IV
Papa.
MILKA
SUCHARD
8

Bessie, age 47, seated in the alcove of the white and gold salon, 1911. Her beaded, lace and georgette gown shows her innate sense of style. Her slim waist belies the fact that she has born seven children.

Return to Wilderstein

1907

1912

ROBERT, THE THREE GIRLS, TWO maids, and their multiple pieces of luggage sped through the night of October 10, 1907, in the first-class sleeping car toward Paris. After a few hours of savoring the autumn-golden city, they took the express train to LeHavre where they boarded *La Lorraine.* Daisy, who remembered the voyage out and had been yearning to return ever since, was brimming with excitement at the certain knowledge she was at last on her way to Wilderstein.

Bessie, Nummie, Addie, and Harry were at the pier in New York to welcome them, and accompanied them up the river to Rhinebeck. As the girls approached the house, the long rays of the late afternoon sun illuminated the storied windows of the tower and cast magic shadows on the filigreed embrasures and railings of the verandahs. The trees in the park shimmered gold, scarlet, mahogany, and deep green. Scattered sailboats cut through the sparkling river, steering clear of the steam-powered barges and passenger boats. The rounded, burnished mountains, so much friendlier than the craggy, snowcapped Alps, embraced the scene. It was a fairy land. Yet their own mother was smiling by their own front door and that night they would sleep in their own beds at Wilderstein, their home.

They spent those first ecstatic days exploring every corner of the house. They reintroduced themselves to little Fiasac, their Scottish terrier. They stroked the cow and discovered that the bright-eyed, knowing donkey Jennie remembered them. They chased each other to see who first would reach the greenhouse or the carriage house or boat house. They went for spins in the big Orient car. And still they had not seen it all.

Their bliss was Robert's bliss. But as soon as they were properly settled, he rushed off to the city. His mission was to test a 1906 Packard "30" offered for sale by the owner, a clubman Harry knew, for only $1,900. The mileage was low. It drove well. Packard's reputation was excellent. He bought it.

That evening he and Harry celebrated with a dinner at the Racquet Club, shot a little pool, then visited the automobile show where Robert ordered a trunk rest and glass windshield to make his new treasure more complete.

That Packard turned out to be an even greater success than the Orient. In fact, it whetted Robert's appetite for cars. Poring over the latest issue of *The Automobile*, he lighted upon a tempting advertisement for a "3 cylinder Elmore 1907 Model 16, like new, $1300." At the same time, he was attracted to a Ford Runabout—"four cylinders with top in good order." That is what he bought. It would be more than true to its name.

Daisy and the twins spent the glorious autumn romping in the fallen leaves, reading books before a crackling library fire, and getting to know their Montgomery cousins—Grace, Bowne, Peg, and Eglinton—who lived at Wildercliff, almost within shouting distance. Though younger by a few years, they would become lifetime friends. Perhaps as an early birthday present, Addie treated Daisy to an outing in New York City. The highlight was a visit to their 80th Street house. It was then rented, so all they could do was stand before it. But Daisy insisted she remembered every detail.

To be sixteen was exciting enough in itself; having the family together at Wilderstein to celebrate it made it inexpressibly more so. Arthur and Robin, sprung from Exeter for Christmas vacation, arrived on that very day. Nummie came down from Harvard the next. Christmas Day was picture book perfect. After breakfast, they opened stockings in the library. The Montgomery family joined them for the midday feast. At tea time they went to Wildercliff for present giving. In an expansive gesture, Robert gave the boys ten dollars each and the girls five dollars, all in gold coins.

When the boys' vacation was over, the girls continued their carefree existence at Wilderstein, skating on neighboring Ellerslie's pond and skiing in its fields. Bessie, having discovered it was a pleasant way of entertaining her new friends, went motoring in the Packard whenever weather permitted—and sometimes when it did not. Her favorite destination was Poughkeepsie, known as the Queen of the Hudson because of its beauty and bustling prosperity. For Bessie, that meant leisurely shopping and nice teas. Both she and Robert made excursions to the city, usually at different times.

Robert spent the next three months puttering around the house. His most useful project, was installing three up-to-date telephones. Then, on January 27, 1908, he departed for Switzerland, leaving domestic affairs under the management of Bessie and the physical needs of the house and farm in the care of the able Wright. As usual, he neglected to correspond. Bessie, however, wrote weekly. Her first news was that the Packard had broken a

After his family's return to America, Robert usually spent February and March in Switzerland where he enjoyed winter sports with his friends. In this photographic postcard, made in 1908, he poses with Algernon Beauclerk at a mountainside inn.

spring. Her second was that she had engaged an English governess, Miss Albro, who was about thirty-five years of age and could teach the girls German and French as well as calisthenics. Most important to Bessie was that Miss Albro was a gentlewoman, for, she explained, "the children are at an age when they will talk too much to servants if they have not ladies to be with them." Yet, she was willing to have her tray sent up or lunch before or after the family. To be content, all Bessie lacked were her boys. "Girls," she wrote Robert, "are such quiet little things."

Daisy, who missed her father "awfully," wrote more sprightly news. "Three teams are bringing in the ice," she reported. "Fiasac disappeared the other day but we found him the next day." Backstairs life tickled her sense of comedy. "Mary spends most of her evenings in the laundry talking to the watchman & he gets awfully angry with her," she reported. "The other night she made him a bed on one of the tables & he told her he hadn't come here to sleep." As for Miss Albro, Daisy liked studying with her very much. "I am with children of 11 in arithmetic," she confided, "but Miss Albro says I can do 3 years in one if I work hard."

When Robert returned to Wilderstein, his gout was so excruciatingly painful, he was virtually immobilized. But, that gave him a chance to watch the Wilderstein spring unfold. In late April he noted that cherry trees were abloom with white flowers and that the willows and almost everything except the locusts were in leaf. Wright was cutting the lawns with the horse and mower. John McCarty, who had worked on the grounds before their departure for Switzerland in 1897 and had come back as a gardener and watchman, was leveling and edging the paths. Feeling better and beckoned by the river, Robert ordered a steel rowboat. The girls and Arthur spent happy afternoons with him, learning to row and, like Ratty and Mole in

The Wind in the Willows, generally messing about on the water. (When Bessie perceived Arthur was struggling academically, she pronounced him too ill to continue school. His illness did not prevent him from becoming a proficient rower, however, or from running up to the Merritts in the Ford for tennis and lunch with Alan and Ethel, who were near him in age.)

Robert was fifty-two years old on June 5, 1908. Everyone gave him presents. But the most prized was the one he gave himself—a second-hand Packard "24" limousine. This one cost $2,500. At the same time he changed chauffeurs. He was lucky in his choice. John Newman would stay in the Suckleys' employ until after Robert's death when they could no longer afford him; even then, he continued to live in the apartment above the stable in the carriage house, now the garage.

Newman's first week of service was not auspicious, however. The four-cylinder Orient's motor "smashed itself." The Ford suffered a mishap that damaged its wheels. Then the Packard limousine collapsed. All at once it seemed that the family's only reliable vehicles were the Columbia motorcycle and the two ladies' bikes with coaster brakes Robert had just bought. The Packard was completely overhauled—518-¾ hours of work plus parts for a total of $1,395.08. The stress was so great, Robert noted in his day book, that he decided to give up smoking then and there.

In its propaganda about the expense of car ownership, the industry claimed that, on a mileage basis, it was a bargain compared to a horse and carriage. In reality, however, there was no question that the cost was high. First, the machine had to be bought and licensed. Then there was the fuel and, since gas stations had not yet sprung up on every corner, its storage. The gasoline for Robert's cars was shipped from NYC in steel barrels on the Saugerties boat at thirteen cents a gallon, F.O.B. New York. His 260-gallon storage tank and pump cost fifty dollars. Some of his endless small purchases may have been indulgences, but many were not and they added up. Among the expenditures Robert noted were one pair goggles, $1.85; one horn, $3.50; two umbrella coats, $8.50; and a rubber shirt for the chauffeur, no price given. Newman's salary was $90 a month, plus a substantial Christmas bonus, making him Robert's most highly paid employee. The cost of repairs and maintenance, as Robert had already learned the hard way, had a habit of catapulting out of sight. In short, automobiles proclaimed affluence. Both Robert and Bessie were perfectly conscious of that fact. So were their children. For them all, that added a certain luster to the cars themselves.

Labor Day weekend brought "lots of Montgomeries" to Wilderstein.

Above: 1906-1907 "30" Packard. Daisy far left.

Right: Arthur in his 1912 Hudson, which his friend Vincent Astor helped finance.

Below: 1912 Hupmobile "32" Touring Car. Bessie awaiting her driver.

Above: Arthur's used 1907 Sterns.

Left: 1912 Hupmobile "32" Touring Car. Alice Dows in fashionable trousered driving costume, Henry and Harford Powell in straw boater.

Below: Katharine driving Robin's stylish Mercedes.

After that Robert was free to tinker with the house. He removed the panels from the kitchen fence and replaced them with square wire netting. He made plans to improve the kitchen entrance by changing the alignment of the stairs. He began toying with the idea of adding a handsome billiard room leading off the second floor above the porte cochere. Fascinated by the advances in iceboxes, he looked into the latest innovations in refrigerators.

When the autumn of 1908 came, only the twins remained at home to give Robert and Bessie a sense of rooted family. Nummie returned to Harvard and Robin joined him there. Arthur was transferred to the Blake School in Westchester, which, with three children to a teacher, aimed to meet the special needs of each student. (At the same time, Arthur, now eighteen, was given a charge account at Brooks Brothers.) Daisy was enrolled in a college preparatory boarding school conducted by Miss Louisa Low and Miss Edith Heywood in Stamford, Connecticut. Although she was almost seventeen years old, this was the first time Daisy had been surrounded by American girls with similar tastes, abilities and aspirations, if not the long experience of living abroad. (That Daisy had never seen roller-skating and others had never seen ice-skating was a source of amusement to them all.) Daisy liked the routine, but what she enjoyed most were the entertainments the girls themselves got up. For a party with a country fair theme, she costumed herself as a washerwoman and, she triumphantly reported, looked "perfectly frightful." She even enjoyed the school food. "Last night we had the finest things to eat I have ever tasted," she wrote her father. "They are called 'dream cakes' and are simply cheese sandwiches fried in butter and eaten hot. I am going to make some as soon as I get home." Because it would interfere with her studies, Daisy did not go to Wilderstein on weekends. However, she quickly accepted when one of the girls who lived in New Haven invited her to attend the Yale-Harvard football game, one of the great events of the eastern sports season. Needless to say, they had "a very fine time."

Robert was happy that, except for Arthur, his family seemed to be getting on acceptably in America. However, with multiple boarding school and college bills on top of the house and grounds, his cars and boats, his New York City hotels, entertainments, and clubs, his vacations in Switzerland, and the ever-increasing expense of feeding, clothing, and doctoring so large a family, he was having a hard time making ends meet. Although the rent rolls for his properties in New York City and New Jersey each came to over seventeen thousand dollars a year, the stock market on which he had long depended for capital gains was "soft." The currency crisis that would be known as the Panic of 1907 showed no signs of abating. As a result,

Left: Robert and his brother-in-law Harry Montgomery on the south verandah at Wilderstein.

Right: Iceboating on the Hudson River.

Robert was forced to make serious efforts to sell important real estate holdings in Rhinebeck as well as in the city and in New Jersey. That market was "soft," too. He did not change his spending ways, however. Quite the opposite. He joined still another club, the New York Yacht Club. Many of his country neighbors were members.

Despite his clubmanship, it is evident that Robert was becoming increasingly introverted, which may have been what he meant when he scrawled in his daybook, "am victim of growing egotism." While Bessie and the children dashed about the countryside during school vacations, he confined his activities more and more to caring for Wilderstein and to brief trips to New York where his routine was to buy things that could not be found in the country, lunch at the Stock Exchange with Harry, dine with him at the Racquet Club, and attend a revue or spicy play with him in the evening. Although he set up a "desk" in Harry's Wall Street brokerage office, he did not spend much time there. His forays into the city may have helped divert his mind from his financial woes. But they certainly did not solve them.

As would become his practice, Robert escaped to Chateau d'Oex during February and March in 1909. There, when gout permitted, he engaged in the usual rounds of skiing, luging, and walking on the high slopes with his friends, Dobbs, Reuss, and Alioth. He ate his fill of *truite au bleu* and played small stakes billiards at Rosat. He submitted to expensive bridgework on his deteriorating teeth in Geneva.

The twins kept him informed about Wilderstein. Betty inspected the new boiler and said it looked as if it were nearly fixed. Katharine told him that Fiasac had killed a cat under the chicken house and that one of the farmhands had made a pen for the new little calf. Nummie had introduced

her to the thrill of iceboating. "I think it is great fun to turn around full speed and nearly be thrown out of the boat," she gleefully reported. Even Bessie's letters were cheerful. She described Arthur's building a snow castle and Katharine's making fudge. As for herself, she took Betty and Katharine to New York for occasional sprees—a Burton Holmes travel lecture on Japan, an entertainment at the Hippodrome, and, according to Daisy, "rushing around to lunches." In fact, she boldly took a room in a small boarding house on 73d Street near Third Avenue. Her only complaints were that Nummie was not in a literary set at Harvard, and that there was too much drinking and, because so many of the professors were Unitarian, there were no chapel services.

Daisy continued to entertain her father with free-spirited letters. She enthused about an astronomer who had discovered twenty-five comets. She drew a little sketch of an elaborate costume she was making for a fancy dress ball. "I'm getting to be quite a seamstress," she proudly told him. She was pleased, too, with her marks—all As except for a B in English literature. At her cooking lessons, which took place in her Aunt Sophie Langdon's Park Avenue apartment and were taught by the New York Cooking School, she had made delicious tomato soup and Swiss sunshine cakes. The orange charlotte would have been good, too, she reported, if a prankster had not put salt in the sugar canister. From time to time she had also attended concerts at the Philharmonic. An Austrian conductor named Mahler particularly impressed her. To lure her father home, she informed him that the river was open, the lighthouse in action, and the day boats running.

Robert, having decided to focus on improving Wilderstein's pleasure gardens, returned there in time for the spring planting. From the local florist Christian Lawritzen—for whom, in the manner of tight-knit small

Robert displaying his cycling prowess on the Wilderstein tennis court. Arthur interrupts his serve.

towns, Robert held a mortgage—he ordered pansies, lilies of the valley, hollyhocks, geraniums, heliotropes, verbena, and sweet alyssum, as well as peppers, cauliflower, and cabbage, the last perhaps for Wright's kitchen garden. Unlike his more affluent neighbors and relatives—Morton, Merritt, Astor and Elizabeth Lynch, for instance—he had given up all attempt to farm in a major way. His records show that he was buying eggs, butter, and cream from Ellerslie; chickens, vegetables, fruits, and jams from Mansakenning; and milk from the Silver Lake Cooperative Creamery at Clinton Corners. He had, however, commenced bringing the hay fields back. Purchases relating to the land include forty-two loads of crushed stone, twenty-six locust posts, fertilizer, and garden tools. In the fall he would buy seven hundred celery plants from Lawritzen. There is no indication if this was in his own behalf or as a secondary moneymaking project on the part of his farmer.

Concern about his health led Robert to buy a top-of-the-line bathroom scale, the kind used in doctors' offices. Every day he would record his weight, often to the ounce, in his daybook. The rapid fluctuations, between 165 and 195 pounds, indicate that he believed there was a connection between his gout and his avoirdupois; since gout results from a malfunction of the kidneys, it probably was. From time to time, he would weigh the girls. That spring, Daisy weighed in at 136½ pounds, Katharine at 119, and Betty at 120, plump for young women of seventeen and fifteen years of age.

Summertime was a social whirl. All the Suckley children were at home. There were young people about their same ages in the Crosby, Merritt, Hamersley, and Chapman, as well as the Montgomery families. They met almost every day in varying configurations for tennis, a sport that was all the rage in America. One of its chief attractions was that it provided a social opportunity for young men and women to mingle and flirt. They all belonged to the Edgewood Club of Tivoli, which had four splendid clay courts and a must-attend Labor Day tournament, but most of the time they played on their own courts, with lunches and teas and, often on weekends, dancing, to add to the pleasure. The Suckleys had learned to play the game so well at Chateau d'Oex that they were always in demand, a good thing since at Wilderstein they were still making do with a rudimentary mowed area.

With the family going off in all directions—Newman had already taught Daisy and Katharine to drive—it became obvious to Robert that they needed still another motor car. This time he bought a brand new 20 horse power Ford. The purchase was made just in time, for both the Orient and Packard were so unreliable that he sold them for parts. To replace them he had his eye on a Packard five-passenger runabout. Its cost was $4,200.

In midsummer, there must have been an overload of guests, mostly Montgomerys. To preserve the peace, Addie was moved from the southeast room on the second floor to the old nursery on the third. Katharine, whose room it was, went to the small third-floor bedroom overlooking the porte cochere. Daisy took the third floor tower room, directly over her father's, which she would occupy until she was well into her nineties. Betty was put in the tiny room on the west side of the third floor. Arthur dropped down to the library where he slept on the sofa. Robin is said to have found a niche in an ironing room in the servants' wing. Nummie, who had developed a knack for removing himself from family tensions, took possession of a room at Wildercliff.

At the same time, Robert reinstalled his billiard table in the Louis XVI salon. For Bessie, to whom the pristine elegance of that room bore social significance, that billiard table must have been the last straw. But there it stayed. At the same time he bought a phonograph. That was easier to accommodate. Music had always been one of the family's most reliable common meeting grounds. The children began to play the piano again, full of moths and other insects as it was, and, with Nummie, Robin, and Robert on the violin, they staged pleasant after-dinner concerts.

Before the family knew it, it was back to school time for the boys and Daisy. Their approaching departures caused little disruption because, for once, they all returned to the previous year's institutions. The supreme excitement of the autumn of 1909, for the whole country as well as the entire length of the river, was the Hudson-Fulton Celebration. The most magnificent event ever staged by the United States, it marked the three hundredth anniversary of Henry Hudson's historic exploration of the river and the centennial anniversary of the first trip of Robert Fulton's steamboat from New York City to Albany and back. Both had changed the course of the nation. Hudson's river became the major northern route to the immense Mississippi River watershed. Fulton's steamboat revolutionized waterborne transportation throughout the world and underscored Americans' genius for invention. The long-planned festivities were international in scope. Nations from around the world sent their warships, their monarchs, their top politicians and private citizens. Towns, villages, and institutions from New York City to Albany joined the fanfare. Nobody, not even the Europeans, had witnessed anything quite like it.

The Suckleys enjoyed the celebration from decidedly privileged positions. They viewed the naval parade from the decks of Astor's fabulous

Katharine in the stern of the Suckley's 30-foot launch *Ellide* with Jack Astor's mighty *Nourmahal* as a backdrop. A comic collage, one of many crafted by the girls.

luxury yacht, the *Nourmahal*. As a member of the New York Yacht Club, Robert received an invitation to its reception for the United States Fleet commander. They saw the army parade from the Metropolitan Club at 59th Street and Fifth Avenue and the historical parade from the Langdons' apartment. Robert and Bessie attended the Society of Colonial Wars dinner at Delmonico's. When the events moved up river, they again boarded Astor's *Nourmahal* to join the rally of pleasure and excursion boats at Newburgh. For Wilderstein's contribution, Robert asked Wright to raise a twenty-six-foot flagpole on the roof. When the replicas of Hudson's Half Moon and Fulton's North River Steamboat were received with gun boats, salutes, and speeches at the Livingston estate, Clermont, everyone except Robert went early in the morning to an island owned by the Crugers, south of Clermont, to see the boats start off. Captain Zabriskie's Blithewood Light Infantry turned out with a band and fired a salute. For the Suckleys, the grand finale was the magnificent display of fireworks over the river put on by Jack Astor at Ferncliff.

Fall progressed with Robert and Bessie making frequent trips to New York City, usually at different times and with different objectives. However, for their twenty-fifth wedding anniversary Robert took Bessie to a spell-binding Fritz Kreisler concert. He also bought her a silver demitasse coffee service and a miniature silver screen to adorn the tea table on the verandah. Bessie treated herself to a new evening wardrobe: three expensive gowns and a beautiful opera coat. Robert refurbished himself with a fine tuxedo, a Norfolk jacket, and knickerbockers.

Daisy was thriving at Miss Low's and Miss Heywood's. She wrote a paper on Alexander the Great, and tackled Cicero and Virgil at the same time. While studying, she ate a mysterious concoction called "brew," as well as bananas, peanut brittle, and oranges in large quantities. She was elected to the committee for entertainments in her house, vice president of her sorority, and treasurer of her class. She visited a new friend, Ninon Newton, at the Newtons' animal-populated country place in Ridgefield, Connecticut. For her weekending, Robert presented her with a fine monogrammed suitcase. "It's a beauty," she told him. "I have been showing it to everybody." Nummie sent her a tempting postcard of the Harvard football team with the message, "These are the fellows who are going to beat Dartmouth tomorrow and Yale next Saturday," Daisy wrote her father. "It shows true college spirit, I wish I could be there." She found time, however, to help entertain at cousin Helen Langdon's tea and to dance at her coming-out party.

When Bessie started agitating about Daisy's health, Daisy took a firm stance. "Please stop worrying about me as I am flourishing," she patiently told her. "I have put on my flannels, wear a sweater outside, take my pills, my apples and my rest begins tomorrow." Unsatisfied, Bessie went after the school's water supply. "Miss Heywood says she had the Stamford water analyzed and the state chemical man said it was perfectly all right," Daisy retorted. "But to make it still safer she filters it and in the autumn everybody has bottled water. The milk also comes in bottles from the state inspector's farms, so really there doesn't seem to be anything to worry about."

Robert, as was his habit, remained aloof from these real or imagined problems. He was blissfully immersed in converting the electrical system from direct to alternating current and to bringing it to more rooms in the house. This required extensive rewiring. On New Year's eve the miracle happened. Shortly after dark, Robert threw a switch and the electric light went on—four illuminated bulbs in the dining room, four in the drawing room, and three in the griffin-supported globe on the hall newel post. The entire family was enthralled.

In fact, so successful were the lights that the year 1910 at Wilderstein might be called the year of electricity. Although Robert spent his usual two months in Switzerland, he laid out the additional work so well that, while he was away, it progressed with no serious hitch. "I am writing this letter with the jointed lamp lighting it," Betty informed him soon after he left for Europe. "The lights in here, (library) are all put in, and the switchboard has been installed. The electricians have started to put the lights in upstairs, all those in the cellar are ready and it is very useful to have them when I have to get the cats."

Working upward, electricity was extended to the garret and tower and finally outward to the carriage house. To make full use of all that reliable current, Robert bought an electric kettle and coffee pot and a Sturtevant vacuum cleaner. He proudly cooked both lunch and supper for himself on his new electric stove—"eggs, sausages and toasted bread, both times," when Bessie was in New York and the cook on vacation.

Nummie graduated from Harvard on June 23, 1910. It was only in response to a desperate plea from Daisy that Robert controlled his aversion to social crowds to attend the festivities. He took Harry with him for support and, rather than stay with other members of the family, spent the night in Robin's rooms. They breakfasted at Nummie's undergraduate club and lunched with him at the Hasty Pudding Club. Undoubtedly Robert was proud of his graduate, but the moment he could get away he and Harry headed for the train station.

Summer was again a banner year for parties, for just about everybody. Daisy was already a "superb" dancer—the strongest compliment bestowed upon her by her mother. Arthur was very good, too. The twins were learning and loved it. In mid-July, Bessie prevailed on Robert to put on a formal dinner for twelve, the seating plan of which Robert carefully sketched in his daybook. She gave a luncheon in early September for which he also recorded the seating. What she did about the billiard table in the salon is not recorded. Later in the month they entertained the children's friends—"2 Dows, 2 Huntingtons, 4 Montgomerys, 1 Zabriskie, 1 boy Chapman, Mrs. Zabriskie, Elizabeth Lynch, Mr. Chapman." At that event the Suckleys and Montgomerys put on a play they had written themselves, the main characters of which were Mr. and Mrs. Punch and a dwarf. Two days later the Merritts followed suit with still another party. Informal mingling with the "river people" filled other days. When Daisy lunched with Kitty Hamersley at Maizefield, her brother Gordon brought her home. "They were both pretty well blacked up as one of the roads had been freshly oiled and his machine had no mud guards," Robert acidly commented. "Her white dress is probably ruined in spite of the dust coat she wore."

Peg Montgomery and Kitty Hamersley (seated); Betty, Daisy, Helen Langdon and Katharine (standing). Photographic postcard, 1911.

Only the absence of Nummie and Robin for most of the summer created a void. After graduation, Nummie, did what his grandfather and his father had done before him, albeit in a less structured way. After visiting a classmate at his game preserve in New Hampshire and tasting a little adventure in Canada, he toured Europe. First he traveled in England and then in Italy, where he was surprised to find he could speak, but not understand the language. Robin, who needed extra credit to remain at Harvard, went off to its engineering camp at Squam Lake in New Hampshire.

Eager as always to keep up with the latest inventions, Robert made a special trip to Sheepshead Bay, Long Island, to see the Curtiss aviation exhibition. That May, Curtiss had flown from Albany to New York, stopping once for fuel in Poughkeepsie. A Curtiss plane would fly the first sack of mail in the fall. The following year, one would take off from the water. Bessie's spree consisted of an autumn trip to Cambridge to check up on Robin and Arthur, both of whom were now at Harvard. She took the twins and rented a little apartment. They did the round of museums and, not to be outdone by Robert, they, too, attended an aviation exhibition, that of the Wright brothers and the Frenchman Blériot.

That October, the twins at last shed their governess. The school Bessie chose for them was conducted by a Miss Bangs and a Miss Whiton in the exclusive Riverdale section of the Bronx. It was "a most desirable place in every way for quiet children like ours and *not at all* a fashionable school, but only an exceedingly nice one," she had assured Robert. It placed children not in graded classes, but at the level for which they were prepared. Moreover, she could visit them easily on her way to the city. To make sure the twins would not be homesick, she persuaded Harry to send Peg and Grace there, too. She then removed Daisy from Miss Low's and enrolled her at Miss Bangs' to watch over them all. Not being partial to the girls, this was no wrench for Bessie. Moreover, it left her free to lead her own social life as she had done in Geneva. Suddenly, the strategy behind her attacks on the Stamford water system became crystal clear. The change could only have been a terrible blow for Daisy. However, as she had often done, Daisy accepted the assignment and gracefully made the best of it.

Robert's winter 1911 vacation in Switzerland was a special pleasure. Nummie, who had played on in Europe, joined him there to take part in the international bobsled competition, held on the La Cresta run at St. Moritz. From the outset Nummie was favored to win the event. He took three trophies, then, in an effort to rebreak the record he had just broken, he cometed off the track. His life was never in danger, but he could not make the championship run the next day. To Robert, Nummie was, nonetheless, a hero. Like many fathers, Robert was beginning to live through his eldest son. Strong in body and mind, Nummie possessed the spirit of a competitor. Although he lacked the high-pitched enthusiasm for cars that his brothers exhibited and was an appreciator rather than a player of music, he had graduated from Harvard, secured a job with a reputable Boston financial house, and enjoyed an attractive circle of friends who invited him to spend weekends at their families' country places. Equally important, while remaining affectionate and teasing, he had become adroit at keeping his mother at bay.

Robert's emotional investment in Nummie became even more acute when he returned to Chateau d'Oex to find a long letter from Robin informing him that he had not passed the hard courses at engineering camp and had been dropped—"immediately so"—from Harvard. A heart-rending *mea culpa*, full of anguish and conflicting values, it expressed in one resounding outburst the cost to the Suckley children of the unstable family life and fragmented education they had endured during their residency abroad. Robin and Arthur were especially ill-equipped to enter the American educational system, for, along with European accents and mannerisms, they had absorbed Europeans' belittling attitude toward their countrymen.

"I attribute my miserable failure to the three years I spent at Exeter... a school made up of Western asphalt diggers," Robin began. "I regarded them as something so entirely apart that I never thought their good opinion was worth having. I am very sorry now that I thought this for I see now how mistaken I was... I wish now that I had been a grind, for that at least would have been one 'interest.'" Instead, he continued to live alone in a crowd. Because of his health, he had not been able to join in baseball or football. At Harvard he had begun to like his classmates more and they to like him. In fact, he declared, that autumn he had started out with a confidence he had never before experienced. Then, finding lessons comparatively easy, "a sort of horrible, bored, suppressive feeling came over me which prevented me from having the slightest ambition or anxiety, or interest in anything that was happening or was going to happen."

Robin was obviously profoundly depressed. The years of his mother's "can't do," countered only by his father's feeble attempts to buttress his abilities in chemistry, mechanics, and music, had taken their toll. Now that the axe had fallen, he woke up to the myriad advantages he would forego by leaving college. "You can hardly realize how important my standing will be,

if I ever live in New York," he went on, "for almost all the New Yorkers that I know well at present belong to the Union Club or are waiting for it. And of course you know better than I could that success in business in New York is largely dependent on one's friends." Abruptly shifting gears, he issued a plea for money to pay current bills and a reminder that he had given almost all his furniture to Arthur. He also wanted enough Harris tweed for two or three suits, and tailor money to have it made up; his preference was for a pattern that did not have too much yellow in it. In addition, he listed the parts needed to keep the F.N. motorcycle running, "for even if I am not to use it myself this summer, N. and Arthur could." However, the best way of solving the "independent transport" problem, he told his father, was for him to bring back "two pair of the German Army road shakers, much improved recently." Returning to the here and now, he concluded, "Remember me to Nummie. We were very glad to hear of his Cresta records."

Daisy graduated from Miss Bangs' and Miss Whiton's on June 2, 1911, an honor roll student with a diploma in classical studies. Perhaps to reward her patience and perseverance, Robert allowed her to tour Europe with Peg and Addie. She crossed the ocean with her father, who took that opportunity to get away, too, and with Arthur, whom Bessie was sending to the Gland sanitarium for still another series of digestive tract treatments. Daisy's itinerary included a meet-up with Peg and Addie at Interlaken, a visitation of their old haunts in Geneva, a dip into Italy, a few days with Robert at Chateau d'Oex and, just before they returned home, a literary tour in Great Britain. Fifteen-year-old Peg, bubbling with carefree merriment and fun, was the best possible company. They had a glorious time.

Daisy would need her memories of that stimulating interlude, for in the fall Bessie sent her back to Miss Bangs' and Miss Whiton's, purportedly to study for the difficult Bryn Mawr college entrance examinations, but primarily to act as guardian for the twins. Even with Daisy on hand, Bessie could not resist sending orders to the headmistresses. "I wish you would not write Miss Bangs and Whiton about everything," Daisy, soon to be twenty, protested. "We are old enough to be told things ourselves and not have a nurse running after us." To display her independence, she flaunted the "frivolity" Bessie so mistrusted. "My white furs and white cloth coat are in the upstairs closet," she told her. "I will need them for Mrs. More's dance next Friday."

Daisy on her graduation from Miss Bangs' and Miss Whiton's School for Girls, in the Riverdale section of the Bronx. . Katharine cautioned her mother not to forget to send the expected sheaf of roses. June 2, 1911.

Robert Bowne Suckley, Jr. Self-designated "official photograph."
Photograph by Aram Studio, Inc., New York, 1917.

Living with a Legacy

1912 — 1921

NUMMIE MOVED TO NEW YORK City in the winter of 1912, having been offered a job in a Wall Street banking outfit. He and Robin set up housekeeping at 41 East 80th Street, which (unfortunately, from Robert's point of view) was not rented. They were precarious co-occupants for Robin was prone to locking his brother out. Whenever there was snow or the promise of iceboating, they weekended at Wilderstein, where, with Robert in Europe, Bessie happily reigned. Her way of sharing their sporting life was to put on grand iceboaters' teas.

Arthur was at Harvard doing the best he could. His chief comfort was a second-hand Hudson automobile that he had bought with financial help from Vincent Astor, Jack's son, who had returned from England and become his friend. However, it was not long before Arthur failed, without reprieve, at Harvard. He thought, perhaps, of taking a half or whole year at Columbia, then trying to reenter Harvard for his senior year, but, realistically, the outlook was bleak.

Robert's way of dealing with the crisis, when he returned to Wilderstein from Europe limping with gout, was to immerse himself in projects of a concrete, useful and somewhat more controllable nature. He had a man up from New York to install an electric clock on the north wall of the great stairwell that would satisfy his desire to know the time with perfect accuracy. Soon he ran secondary electric clocks to the kitchen and the stable. One of his favorite occupations was checking them to the second against his fine Swiss pocket watch, then noting the disparity in his daybook. He replaced the light under the porte cochere with a forty-watt Sunbeam tungsten bulb, had the kitchen chimney fixed, leveled the corners of the tennis court and limed the garden. He "rejuvenated" the Packard and sent the *Ellide* to Buckhout's to have the motor overhauled. Building on the cooperative arrangement he had with Harry for the improvement of

Wildercliff, he promised to stand the expense of a new hot water heater, with Harry paying him ten percent interest on the $350 it would cost.

Stimulated by these accomplishments, he went on a major building spree. He obviously needed a special room for his billiard table. He asked his brother-in-law Alan Montgomery, an architect, to help him with the design. For a starting point he rooted out the drawing of the east elevation Downing Vaux had made twenty years before. He and Alan spent many happy hours enlarging its scope. It would include a fine room over the library as well. The style of the exterior was Tudoresque.

While Robert was immersed in improvements, the family socialized in its usual manner. There was only one great exception, the death of Jack Astor. He had finally divorced Ava Willing, then married an eighteen-year-old beauty of unexalted origin. To protect her from the snubs of his relatives and most of his friends, he took her abroad. For their return passage in February 1912, he engaged passage on the *Titanic*. Astor managed to obtain a place for his wife, who was pregnant, on the next-to-last lifeboat. He went down with the ship. Robert was truly shaken. In addition to enjoying Astor's liberal hospitality, Robert had shared a fascination for mechanical and technological innovation with him. Vincent became his father's sole heir. Conservatively estimated, the estate was worth $92 million. Soon, Arthur was racing around with him in a Lancia automobile capable of doing 120 miles an hour.

During the summer, Robert at last got around to replacing Wilderstein's mowed-grass tennis court with a professionally built clay tennis court. The boys, who had long urged him to do so, did not stay around to watch the construction. In early July, Robin left for the Harvard engineering camp, and Nummie for destination unknown, "probably for Detroit," Robert jotted in his daybook, obliquely referring to a fascinating young woman from that city who had recently visited the Lynches. While the old tennis court was torn up, Bessie put on a little drawing class for the girls and their friends and Elizabeth Lynch organized a sewing class. Robert bought a Hupmobile 32 tonneau and drove it 225 miles in five days. The new court was at last ready to play on in early September. Katharine challenged her father to a match and won.

Daisy, who, much to her father's joy, had passed the entrance exams to Bryn Mawr in the spring, entered the college at the end of the month. Her first letters home dance with excitement. After assuring her mother that she was "plentifully supplied with all warm underwear and 'overwear'," she described how much she was enjoying her studies, especially her history of

Snapshot of Robert and "the bunch" by the gazebo near the Wilderstein tennis court, June 6, 1914. Robert, Daisy (just returned from Bryn Mawr College), twin, Peg, twin.

art lessons. "The teacher is fascinating and is fast imbuing me with quite an aesthetic pleasure in the frightful people of sculpture and painting. The library here is wonderful," she went on. "They have over 70 thousand volumes and a delightful reading room." Her fellow students were extraordinarily friendly, the upper classes giving the new girls teas almost every day. Daisy and her roommate occupied a suite. She had bought a beautiful Morris chair for twelve dollars, and hangings for both bedroom doors for eight dollars. Her roommate had a desk, a bookcase, and a wicker chair. A carpet and tea table were coming. They were going to "the pike (meaning the village!)" to order some ferns for the window shelves. "I have a checkbook, and I made my first check out yesterday," she triumphantly concluded. On a crammed and essentially taunting penny post card, she informed Bessie that her physical examination was "very thorough and satisfactory." The doctor tested her heart carefully when she told him it was supposed to be weak and he said it was "in *perfect* condition." She was particularly proud that she had tested ninth in strength of her class of 125. To excite her mother still further, she announced that the president of the college,

M. Carey Thomas, was "a suffragist and an admirer of [Theodore] Roosevelt!!" (This was the year the former Republican president ran as a progressive "Bull Moose" against the incumbent president, William Howard Taft, and lost.)

It is astonishing that the Suckleys chose Bryn Mawr for Daisy. M. Carey Thomas was a liberated woman, albeit a well-born one. She was a force among college presidents, of men's as well as women's institutions. She saw no reason why women should not be as widely and deeply educated as men, nor why they could not address the broader issues confronting the nation just as well. Not for her the soft, guiding voice at the hearthside, whose only means of public expression was through a husband, father or brother. She possessed a discriminating social conscience and expected her girls to develop one, too. At the same time, she ran a tight ship educationally. Her 70,000-volume library with its comfortable reading room speaks for itself.

Arthur, cowboy polo player at Mesa, Arizona, 1913

It was undoubtedly Robert who chose Bryn Mawr. Like Harvard, it was prestigious. Radcliffe might have been an option, but the family had not had much success in Cambridge of late. Bessie may have acquiesced because her family had deep roots in Philadelphia, principally the Chews, whose coat of arms embellished one of Wilderstein's dining room windows. Moreover, she had found a suitable boarding school for the twins in Chestnut Hill, a close suburb of Philadelphia, where, in her free time, Daisy could keep an eye on them. She only wished the school's curriculum was not geared to sending girls to college.

Katharine echoed her mother's sentiments. "This is a place for working allright! either exercising or studying all the time and hardly anytime for private duties." She especially hated algebra. She liked the basketball, but was disgusted with the caliber of her classmates' tennis—"a stringless racket serves perfectly well," is how she put it. Betty sloughed off the study part. What they both liked was Philadelphia—the shopping, good music, theater

Inscribed by Daisy: "Isabelle Ninon Newton, age $15\frac{10}{12}$; Katharine Bowne Suckley, age $18\frac{7}{12}$," (standing); "Elizabeth Montgomery Suckley, age $18\frac{7}{12}$; Margaret Lynch Montgomery, age $17\frac{1}{12}$" (seated).

and the proximity to New York City. What they did not like was that their mother sent them scratchy, starched cotton underwear when silk lingerie was all the vogue.

Robin had departed for "the West" after his stint at Squam Lake. Arthur went to Mesa, Arizona, in early October, a destination which may have been chosen for him because the climate was known to be beneficial for sufferers of respiratory problems. He loved it. Arizona was still a frontier. It had just been admitted to the Union. As the West was filling up, it had become a nostalgic symbol for freedom and individuality. The ranch on which he lived seems to have had some claim to be a school. But what he enjoyed most was polo, at which he became proficient. Robin, meanwhile, had made his way to El Paso, Texas, taking in western life as it came along. "You must be wondering where I'm going and when I'm coming back," he wrote. "I do not know myself. I may start for a ranch near Mexico City this evening, or I may take the train for New Orleans and then a boat for home, or I may go just a little distance into Mexico." What he did do is go to Mexico, a dangerous place at that time due to revolutionary fever.

There, much to Daisy's horror, he attended a bullfight.

Robert sat at home at Wilderstein, listening to the katydids singing. He transformed the Ford J by giving it an express body and a self-starting ignition. On his chainless bike, he rode almost to the Hudson River Insane Asylum, on the outskirts of Poughkeepsie. Cycling served a twofold purpose: it was a way of keeping his weight down and it got him out of the house. Addie and Nettie were paying one of their extended visits. Katharine sympathized with her father. "I am glad the aunts have quieted down of late and are not working on their nerves," she told her father. In December, to increase usable space, important for everyone's indoor pleasure, Robert set Wright to putting up a glass enclosure on the west verandah, perhaps hoping to approximate Rosat's sun room. Although the heating system Robert devised diverted so much steam from the house radiators that it was used only once, Bessie thought it was a lovely addition. She was right.

Daisy was at Bryn Mawr for her twenty-first birthday. Apparently, the family took little notice of the event. The only record that it occurred is in Robert's daybook, which simply states that she was twenty-one that day. That the following year, when she was twenty-two, Daisy declared in a rare outburst of temper that no one should celebrate a birthday after age twenty-one, suggests that she may have been hurt by her family's neglect of her twenty-first. Still, she was overjoyed when everyone except Arthur congregated at Wilderstein for Christmas. Arthur made his presence known by writing that he did not mind their using his Hudson automobile as long as they kept it in good working order.

After New Year's Day 1913 everyone again scattered. "This living in different places is dreadful and breaks up the family very sadly," Daisy wrote from Bryn Mawr, for once expressing her conflicted emotions. However, Katharine, who was fast developing a thick skin as far as her mother's meddling was concerned, was less nostalgic. "I feel much more energetic at school than I ever do at home and hardly ever have a cold," she told her. "I think it's because here you don't have time to think about yourself so much and there is less occasion of being selfish and self-centered."

Increasingly the girls found a refuge in their Montgomery cousins. They had become what they called "a bunch," going to movies, dances, and tennis matches together, attending each others' school performances, clowning around, and sharing each other's woes. They wrote long, silly letters, baring their social and inner lives. They were constantly inventing names for each other. Betty was "Snooks," Katharine "cat" and "squal"; Daisy was "box," or

"B.O.X." or "trunk." Grace was "Mike," Peg was "Pete" or "Peggoty." (They even called their aged cousin Elizabeth Lynch "rabbit" or "Rab" for short.) One letter from Grace to Katharine begins: "Well now you old idiot, how are you? You hideous pink-eyed rabbit, you frightful red-nosed crocodile, why haven't you written me?" A postscript reads: "Three cheers. I am just living for the time five years hence having failed to persuade people to marry us we return to Rhinebeck to eat and go to the movies. Robin said the other day that since people should not look at us we'd be forced to look at each other. Write at once."

This did not stop the "bunch" from making friends outside the family circle. That August, Daisy had a lovely time visiting Frances Olmstead at her family's place in a summer enclave on Squam Lake. There Daisy met all sorts of new people as well as relatives and family connections. That summer she also visited a classmate in Louisville, Kentucky. It was the first time she had been in the South and she was fascinated by its unique landscape and its different traditions. The friend, Mary Lee Hickman, a.k.a. "Hicko," would return with her to visit Wilderstein. Arthur was also gadding about. His focus was Bar Harbor, where he learned to dance the tango and the Turkey Trot, priceless social attainments which he would pass on to his sisters.

Although age, widening acquaintance and differing interests took them afield, all the children felt the pull of Wilderstein. The Thanksgiving holiday had always been a special get-together time. That year it was somewhat muted. Bessie's dire warnings about Robin's fragility had at last been vindicated. He had undergone a life-threatening appendectomy in the fall and still had not fully recovered. In addition, "poor little Fiasac," who had taken

Daisy and Bryn Mawr classmate Mary Lee Hickman aboard the *Ellide*.

to wandering and picking fights with other dogs, disappeared. Everyone at Wilderstein and at Wildercliff, too, searched and inquired fruitlessly. Two weeks later a railroad worker found his dismembered head and one forepaw, just south of the Wilderstein track crossing. Robin, who had a pronounced sardonic streak, was all for having his head stuffed and mounted. Horrified, Daisy organized a prompt family veto. Instead, they acquired a six-month-old Scottish terrier whom they named Trossac. Despite Daisy's patient efforts to train him, he would grow into as fierce a fighter as the lamented Fiasac.

While at Rosat in the winter of 1914, Robert had a brand new activity to occupy him—getting up his federal income tax. Congress had passed the bill the previous year. Despite the fact that the relationship between his income and his expenditures was far from encouraging, he actually reveled in pulling the figures together. Perhaps it made him feel like his Uncle Rutsen, or his father, to be so minutely engaged in reviewing his accounts.

Robert had a second engaging activity that may or may not have been new. That some tender relationship existed in his life seems evident by an early entry in his February daybook that simply states "Diary of Marie Baskirtsiff for une amie." Whether she was the Miss "X" with whom he had walked and lunched the previous year, or Miss Bickett who took his photograph and sent him cards, or some other will never be known. Nor will the degree of their friendship. But when he returned to the United States he would take a private letterbox at the Yacht Club, where he would receive especially personal mail.

Meanwhile, Bessie was more on edge than ever. All three boys were camping out at 80th Street and, left on her own at Wilderstein, she convinced herself that without their mother to look after them, they would soon be on the road to perdition, if not death. Sitting on the side of her bed at four o'clock in the morning, she wrote Robert:

> How I wish I could be with the boys at 80th St. Just have my room there. They are drifting about and homeless in that place now. You can not imagine how wrong it is not to give a home to them. They are not robust as you were and have a mother who is alive and able to be with them and at least give them a place to come to with some comfort, instead of that cheerless house which they naturally avoid in the evening. Nummy is not looking very well nor Arthur either and Robin always was very delicate. I do fear their getting into the way of taking stimulants to keep up, which they probably do now. ...Only a slight expense would establish me in a room there. I would be willing to use a

Henry as a young man about town. Multiple image photographic postcard.

> little of my own money, if I found it necessary… I do not think they would want to go out often if they had a home for they are all disposed to be very tired in the late afternoon.

In reality, the boys were leading a casual, indulgent life—not too different from that Robert had pursued at their age. They frequented the Harvard Club and various unspecified entertainments. Arthur was playing the stock market and had his eye on a little $2500 Bugatti. Robin bought a stylish old Mercedes to make a splash in town and in the country. Nummie put on a series of house parties at Wilderstein in which Grace Eliot, the granddaughter of Harvard's famous president and Daisy's friend from Swiss days, occupied a prominent role. Robin converted the tennis court into an ice skating rink.

If they hoped to sidestep their mother when they leased a small apartment at 43 Fifth Avenue for two months, they were misguided. Bessie sent them one of the maids and moved in herself. Wilderstein was effectively closed. Only the cook, a maid, and the laundress remained to hold the fort. Nummie had long pleaded with his father to do just that, both to save the expense of heating Wilderstein and to establish a more solid social footing in the city. It simply did not work out as he had imagined. In fact, 43 Fifth Avenue was only the first of a series of apartments Bessie would rent each winter, both to put her in a better position to supervise her boys' lives and to lead her own.

Daisy was as happy as could be at Bryn Mawr, enjoying new friends and pursuing new lines of thought. One of her major projects was a long report on "Women and Child Labor in the United States." Her favorite recreation was going to dances in her stylish white silk dress adorned with shimmering spangles.

Bessie did not care to see the twins following in Daisy's footsteps and did everything in her power to dissuade them from attempting college. In this she had the ardent collaboration of Nettie. "I am rather sorry you are still expecting to go to college in the fall, as I know how much it will help to have you at home, and how much your mother needs that help and care, and brightness of young life would cheer her up," she wrote Katharine. In fact, neither of the twins had any desire to go to Bryn Mawr. Katharine had already dropped algebra as being beyond her capabilities. Her abiding interests were art and music. Betty had never been a scholar. She could not wait to "pitch the wretched books into the fire and never look at them again." Still, both prized their independence too much to bury themselves in their mother's skirts, whether it be in the city or at Wilderstein.

The obvious alternative was marriage. All the Suckley children were now in their twenties. The time was ripe, if not overripe by the standards of the day, for the girls, especially, to wed. The social activities of that spring were a constant reminder of that fact. Helen Huntington and Vincent Astor were married on April 30, a subdued ceremony in some respects because Vincent was in a wheelchair, still not recovered from a severe case of mumps. Helen, the Langdon cousin who was Daisy's age, married in May. According to Katharine, the Suckleys and Montgomerys bunched together as usual and had a grand time. (This marriage would have a lifetime significance for the Suckleys. Helen's five girls, nicknamed the Brownies because their father's name was Brown, would become lifelong younger friends of Daisy and Betty. The three who were still alive when Daisy was in her late nineties made Wilderstein vibrant with sparkling laughter from the moment they stepped over the threshold.) Anne Rogers' wedding at the family's estate Crumwold Hall in Hyde Park was one of the fabulous events of the season. There were hundreds of guests, many of them brought by special train from New York. In addition, Kitty Hamersley was engaged. There were, however, no signs of any of the Suckley children marrying.

Henry with Model No. 4 Folding Kodak camera.

The Astors, Vincent and Helen, put on the usual Fourth of July fireworks display followed by a little dance at Ferncliff. The Hamersleys, having pulled down Bessie's great-grandfather's house at Annandale, were building an imposing riverfront mansion next to the Zabriskies' Blithewood. The girls played a little desultory golf in Staatsburg. When the Olmsteads visited the Mongomerys at Wildercliff, Robin rushed Frances which "the bunch" found "too humorous for words." Peg and Daisy then visited the Olmsteads at Squam Lake. They had an even better time than the previous year—tennis, dancing, charming Kentuckians. That Nummie was at Squam Lake, too, added to their gaiety. In the "it's a small world" category of surprises, he ran into a La Villa classmate, who gave them all a very fine party.

In every way it seemed like just another carefree summer. There was, however, a profound difference. In the first week of August 1914, Germany declared war on Russia and France, invaded Belgium, and commenced establishing control of the seas surrounding Great Britain. In response, Great Britain declared war on Germany. The war would transform the Suckley family, but at the time, the only notation of its outbreak in Robert's daybooks was on July 31: "The NY Stock Exchange did not open this morning. Germany is mobilizing."

Henry, departing to serve in the American Field Service Ambulance Corps in France.

For Nummie, however, it was a turning point. Almost immediately, he signed up with the American Field Service, which was organizing an automobile ambulance corps in France. He was the ideal volunteer. He understood European ways of doing things. He was proficient in German and French and had a passable understanding of Italian. His knowledge of how automobiles operated was first-rate. He was mature—twenty-eight years old—and possessed a commanding physical presence. He was well acquainted with illness. Moreover, he had had some military training: he belonged to a reserve regiment that had been in line to be sent to Mexico the previous year when the United States invaded that country to protect its business interests. Almost as important, he was intimate with people who could donate money and supplies. Mrs. Morton had already requested that he drive the ambulance she had funded. Later, members of the New York Stock Exchange, at the urging of Harry, would buy a squadron of twenty-five ambulances which he would command on the eastern front.

Henry, as Nummie now liked to be called (he had been signing his letters HMS for some time), spent most of January 1915 at Wilderstein, where he and his father and the twins had very good iceboating. When the wind was not too high they even took Trossac along. Then, at ten o'clock on the morning of January 31, he sailed on the American steamship *Chicago* to take up his duties in France. He stayed in close touch with all his family, both by letter and through the photographs he took with the camera "Peggoty" and Katharine gave him as a going-away present. Stationed at the American Hospital at Neuilly-sur-Seine, his first assignment was to get eight Ford cars up and running. According to Robert, he was able to put two together in a day. In April he was sent to a little village, "no bigger than Rhinecliff," in the Vosges mountains. His job was to carry wounded soldiers from the front lines in Germany back into France. The distance was twenty miles over dangerous terrain, but, he wrote his mother, "My health has never been better and I am having a most interesting time." By August he had acquired a position of some responsibility and become so attached to his work that he decided to stay all winter. His only disappointment was that he had just missed being in the right location to get a *croix de guerre.* "It

Henry's photograph of American Field Service ambulances in France.

is quite a pretty medal," he wrote Katharine, "and since the occasion won't arise again in a hundred years, I guess I'll have to do without it."

In September, he was stationed near Dijon. "Stevo, the Monk" (Stephen Galatti), a Harvard classmate whom he had persuaded to join the ambulance corps, was there with two other college intimates. The Germans were continually attempting futile attacks, and once a week the corpsmen had some pretty hard work, but for the most part he thought things would remain relatively calm. He enclosed several photographs in his letters home, one showing that he had "not been worn away by the vast game in which I am the humblest of pawns." His Christmas letter told a different tale. Writing in his dirty ambulance, waiting for another trip down a road turned into a sea of mud by torrential rains, he told his mother of daily bombardments, attacks, counter attacks and awful carnage. Just before the courier took off for Paris, he added, "very strange New Year's eve and nothing but rain."

The family carried on at Wilderstein. For some reason never fully disclosed, Daisy had not returned to Bryn Mawr the previous fall. In later years, she said she had struck a bargain with her parents: she would go to college and study seriously for two years to satisfy her father, then come home to satisfy her mother. Still, she went back for special events, including the graduation of her class, which must have been a particularly poignant time for her. In later years she always spoke of her time at Bryn Mawr glowingly. She would stay in touch with the friends she made there—and their children—all her life. To her great credit, she did not agonize over

Henry (far right) and his squadron of ambulance drivers soon to depart for the Eastern Front, January 1917. (Henry's uniforms have been preserved in the Wilderstein collections.)

Bryn Mawr Class Day, June 1916. Daisy marked herself, third from left top row, and Helvetia Orr, top row far right, with X's.

whatever decision led to her leaving. As she had done so many times before, she simply treasured the experience and got on with the life that was at hand.

That winter, it was spending time at Wilderstein with her father, who because of the danger from submarines had canceled his annual trip to Switzerland. The twins were at home, too. They skated and skied and shared acute mortification when Trossac led their two French bull dog puppies on a hunting expedition to Tracy Dows' wild duck breeding pen. The naughty dogs killed all forty birds without attempting to eat any of them. A few nights later, they returned for eighteen of Dows' hens. Robert sent Daisy to bring the dogs back, then telephoned his sincere regrets and offered to pay Dows whatever he thought right. Amiably, Dows charged five dollars apiece for the ducks and a dollar apiece for the hens. Then, he prudently put a watch over his flock of young turkeys. The problem was, nonetheless, embarrassing, for Robert and Dows were engaged in a protracted legal contest over who owned the property on which the Suckley power station was located.

In clement weather, Robert and the girls worked on the grounds. While Jennie the donkey looked benignly on, they pulled grapevines and poison ivy from the badly deteriorated Umbrella Point gazebo, cleared the marine growth around the Indian rock, and made new paths. "Daisy, Betty and

Grace cleaned the spring of my childhood," Robert noted in his day book. "Two frogs living in it!" For themselves, the girls made a Roman Garden off the walk that led from the house to the stables. So that they could water it, Robert dug down to a pipe from the house cistern that had been laid in 1890. He burned the rubbish around the "Romance" fountain (near the Pinxter Bloom shrub southeast of the house) and gave McCarty some apple seeds to plant. They were from very fine red-and-white apples Robert had eaten on the SS *France*.

The summer was devoted to tennis, golf, dancing, movies, and visiting the Jersey shore. Arthur and Robert bought and sold cars. Robert's latest treasure was a Hupmobile. Arthur went riding on Vincent Astor's hydroplane, then, to improve his eyesight, entered Kellogg's Battle Creek sanitarium to have a bone in his nose that pressed on his optic nerve removed. Robert stoically combated bad teeth, clogged bowels, and weight gain. He labored over his income tax and took up smoking again.

To aid civilian victims of the war, Elizabeth Lynch organized a ladies' sewing circle. Daisy put together a Kimona Club, probably to make bathrobes for convalescing soldiers. What she really yearned to do was to follow Henry to France as a nurse for the American Field Service, but Robert and Bessie would not allow her to do so. However, in May, all the girls joined Mrs. Theodore Roosevelt, Mrs. J. Borden Harriman, Mrs. Richard Aldrich and thousands of business-professional and home-maker women in the patriotic Citizens Preparedness parade up Fifth Avenue.

Otherwise, with the exception of their cousin Bowne, who had volunteered as an ambulance driver, and Ethel Merritt, who had gone as a nurse,

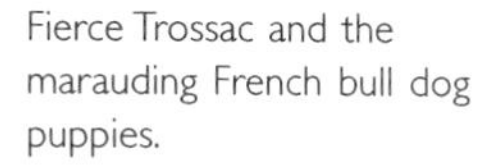
Fierce Trossac and the marauding French bull dog puppies.

Betty. Photograph by Aram Studio, Inc., New York, 1917.

the Suckleys and most of their friends were so focused on their daily pleasures that it almost seemed as if there were no war on and that Henry was not in the thick of it. But that was not so. The family was simply holding its breath. The letters and post cards flowed back and forth. Robert kept careful track of where Henry was stationed and what the fighting conditions were. He read *Four Weeks in the Trenches.*

By the time New Year's 1916 rolled around Robert could not restrain his desire to see Henry and booked passage on an American liner to Bordeaux. They met in Paris, then Henry joined him at Chateau d'Oex for a brief holiday. Each reported on the other to Bessie. Henry told her that Papa was well, but a little lonely. Few of his companions were there. Robert wrote, "HMS's physical & mental attitude is far superior to the petit Nummie vous avez connu. Maintenant il est *un homme!* [Now he is a man.] He weighs 78½ kilos." So buoyant was Robert's mood that he sent Bessie a picture post card of Berne on her birthday with the message, "I wondered if you remembered this scene which nous deux avons regardes le 23 Dec. 1884." [which we enjoyed on our first Christmas together.] Robert and Henry shared some fine dinners in Paris, when Robert was on his way back home.

Soon afterwards, Henry signed up for three more months and contemplated staying a year, if he received the command on the eastern front that he had been promised. "I have had absolutely no signs of the various ills that, you say, life has in store for me," he teased his mother. "Also, note well, I will have none of your so-called abdominal protectors." This was, in part, bravado, for the dangers of war were ever present. That year Victor Chapman, his neighbor, had been killed flying for France in the Lafayette Esquadrille.

Henry's three months stretched into six, during which he was stationed not far from Nancy on the Moselle river. Then, to everyone's inexpressible joy he came home to Wilderstein. He went down to New York to speak before the New York Stock Exchange which, at Harry's urging, had financed a squad of twenty-five ambulances. To Robert's great pride, Nummie performed magnificently, answering every question with confidence and hard information. Toward the end of his leave, he made a quick trip to Detroit. On November 11, he was on his way back to France.

"I will stay as long as I am really needed," he wrote as soon as he safely arrived. "You can't expect, dear Mamma, to have your whole family with you always... Everybody has to live his own life & cannot hope to remain peacefully at home always. My life does not lie at home now, & I feel as if I would be losing a great opportunity if I stayed at home when so much that is vital is going on abroad." In Paris, he focused on getting his squadron ready for work on the eastern front. "Every one of the 25 cars has to be gone over by me & every spark plug catalogued, every tool counted, the numbers of every tire taken." That done, he anxiously awaited orders to entrain for Marseilles, from which the unit, comprised of the ambulances, two supply trucks, a repair car, a kitchen car, and his touring car—"very similar to the one that usually spends the night under the porte-cochere,"—would be shipped to Salonika and driven over the mountains into the Balkans. At Christmastime he was still waiting. "You have probably had snow and ice with skiing and skating," he wrote. "Here nothing but rain. Merry Christmas to you all. Only wish I could be with you for it." On December 27, the orders, at last, came through.

The New York apartment Bessie rented in the winter of 1917 was at 667 Madison Avenue. It was large enough to make a nice retreat for Robert, too. He preferred Wilderstein, where he could enjoy an interlude of peace and quiet, before Bessie's return with Addie and Nettie in tow. Daisy spent much time with him. The others came occasionally for a day or two.

On March 15, Robert was at Wilderstein by himself—the girls were giving a festive opera party in Helen Astor's box—when the faithful John

McCarty died of pneumonia. "Employee 89-97, gardener 1908-16, 1 week ill," he gravely noted in his daybook. The family came up for the funeral and then dispersed. Robert was just settling into his customary routine, when, on March 18, 1917, the always dreaded cablegram came. "HMS at Zemlak, Albania, struck by a fragment of a bomb dropped by aviators. Was taken to hospital at Koritza at once. No hope!" is all his daybook says.

Katharine must have come up as soon as she heard the news for she was with him when he went to New York the next day for a House of Rest meeting. His daybook carefully notes all the other attendees and also that he weighed 184⅛ pounds, that the morning was clear and calm with a stiff frost, and that he ate sausage and hominy for lunch and raw oysters for dinner. It was as if he were willing himself to believe that nothing had changed, that Henry's role as a noncombatant had protected him. Finally, he was compelled to write, "HMS died at 11 a.m. at Koritza, Albania."

Daisy, Betty, and Robin hurried to Wilderstein to comfort their father. Bessie stayed in New York, emotionally frozen. Katharine, Arthur, and the faithful Addie ministered to her as best they could. (Nettie was tormented that illness kept her from going, too.) Letters, cards, and flowers bearing heartfelt sympathy arrived by every mail. Some were from people who had met Henry just once and never forgotten him. Still, Bessie could not bring herself to accept what had happened. Even after she arranged for a memorial service at the Church of the Incarnation, she wrote Robert, "It seems so strange I cannot understand it. Our darling Nummie, how we shall miss him always!" It was only at the end of the month that she was able to face all the poignant memories enfolded at Wilderstein.

For Robert, receiving letters from Henry, sent before he was killed, was one of the hardest trials to bear. The first among them announced his engagement to Betty Miller, the girl he had been visiting in Detroit. "I have been devoted to her for five years. You may ask Cousin Elizabeth about her," is all Henry said about it. Concluding with his usual affectionate banter, the reading of which must have devastated Bessie, Henry joked, "By never wearing my muffler either at waist or throat have avoided all colds & sore throats." When Stephen Galatti sent photographs of Henry's mounded grave in the cemetery at Koritza, his words to his dear mama when he arrived at Salonika became an awful, inescapable reality: "My life does not lie at home now." Its stark cross was inscribed simply, "CI GIT [Here lies] Lieutenant Suckley, Henry, SS. Americain No. 10, Mort pour la France, Mars 18, 1917, 30 ans."

To numb his great grief, Robert enlarged the photograph of Henry taken at sea the previous August and gave copies to close relatives. When Nettie was visiting, they played hymns on violin and piano. Bessie, whom Robert had taken to calling Mama, went through the motions of planting and weeding a vegetable garden. Remaining in the city, Daisy and Katharine volunteered to do clerical work for the National League of Woman's Service. Katharine took a nursing course which involved hands-on practice at the Manhattan Eye and Ear Hospital three times a week. She also took up horseback riding in Central Park, an expensive hobby, she confessed, but it cleared her head. Daisy who had already done her nurse's training, soon returned to Wilderstein, where she kept the household running with Betty's help and learned to can fruit and vegetables. Her first success was rhubarb. She also learned to run a knitting machine, on which she made clothing for refugees.

This hands-on work helped distract Daisy from her pain, but could not alleviate it. To be closer to Henry's memory, she corresponded with Betty Miller. She must have expressed her grief as she could not to any one else. Although Betty wrote, "You seem to know and understand just what I need most," in the end it was she who consoled Daisy. She thought of her as her little sister. "Truly" she said, "I think I am having the easier time of it for it is much easier to bear a grief if you can be alone in it. It must be so hard to see your mother and father suffer." Her final advice to Daisy was, "if

Henry's grave, the military cemetery at Koritza, Albania.

Arthur in the uniform of the American Field Service Ambulance Corps in France. Autumn 1917. (Arthur's uniform is in the Wilderstein collections.)

you ever love a man don't wait to find out what might happen, but marry him right away."

Life did go on, as it must, and not all was mourning. The developing romance of Peg Montgomery and Rupert Anderson, a handsome New Jersey man who worked for a trust company, charmed and delighted them. When Robert learned of their engagement he wrote Katharine, to "tell Peg what Socrates said when asked if it was advisable to marry! that one regretted it whether you did or didn't. He was a misanthrope, however. My experience has been just the other way." The marriage would take place in early October. The youngest of "the bunch," except for Grace, Peg was the first to set up her own household.

The problem before Arthur and Robin at this time was what role to play in the war. Spurred by Germany's military successes and its resumption of unrestricted submarine warfare, the United States had declared war on April 6, 1917. To increase the strength of its armed forces, it instituted a draft. Arthur and Robin registered in early June. Arthur claimed exemption because of physical disability; he was said to weigh only 109 pounds. Then, almost at once, he volunteered for a six-month stint in the American Field Service Ambulance Corps. He sailed for France on August 1. To everyone's relief, he was assigned to an administrative position. It was to match individuals seeking help with the war relief organization that would best provide it, then to check up on how well their needs had been met. "Everyday I thus meet interesting French people who are looking after the great number of refugees and incapacitated soldiers and their families," he wrote his father. He was his own boss, which he enjoyed quite as much as the opportunity to spend a great deal of time in Paris. His fluency in French was, at last, being put to good use.

Robin, as a reservist in the National Guard, was called up for duty in August and sent for basic training to Camp Wadsworth, at Spartanburg,

Robin training for action in the 105th Machine Gun Battalion, Autumn, 1917. (Robin's uniform is in the Wilderstein collections.)

North Carolina. The family watched from the platform of the New York Public Library at Fifth Avenue and Forty-second Street as the unit paraded to the station. At camp, assigned to the 105th Machine Gun Battalion, he formed a wry view of the war. "Germany is like a camel's back awaiting the last straw before breaking," he wrote Katharine. "All the boys are crazy to apply it even if they have to swim. I understand from a trustworthy source that the Kaiser cries all day long and is planning to surrender to the first American appearing at the front. I believe I could take care of it if the family sent me a box with a dozen oranges, some boxes of brown Educator crackers and a pound or so of Swiss cheese and also a few cartons of those very small not-seeded-seedless raisins. The food has become much worse since leaving New York and I have to help it from the outside."

Instead of renting an apartment in New York that winter, Bessie took Betty and Daisy to visit Robin at Spartanburg, where they made themselves comfortable in an attractive house Robin had found for them. Its special advantage was its fireplace and two extra bedrooms that he and his friends could use when they were off duty.

The girls had the time of their lives. "Mama and Betty are at church, and I am here with Robin, Mr. Farnum and Mr. Russell and have just been playing some dreadful ragtimes for them to sing to," Daisy wrote Katharine. Another evening, they were invited to dine in the officers' shack with a newly married couple, who brought along two unmarried friends. After the dinner, fifty men from the company performed vaudeville sketches. The evening ended with a midnight snack in a town restaurant. "The two bach-

Bessie with sewing on the verandah at Wilderstein, 1917.

elors *said* they were coming to see us," Daisy reported to Katharine, "and will ask us to the first regimental dance they have, and also to dinner! We will wait for developments!"

The developments came, not in the form of those two bachelors, but in the elegant person of Lieutenant Littleton C. F. Hambley, a North Carolinian. "Mama is crazy about him as he is awfully good looking," Betty confided to Katharine, but it was Betty who enchanted Hambley. He visited almost every evening and, on Saturdays, put on dinners for the girls with movies and dancing afterwards. Bessie chaperoned them on a weekend excursion to the mountain town of Asheville. As Robin proudly put it, Daisy and Betty were "making a big hit with the fellows, for the first time in their lives they have it all over the other girls."

Those were their gaities. To help the war effort, they took a Red Cross course in making surgical dressings every morning. Two afternoons a week, carefully watched over by older ladies, they served soldiers at the canteen. Then Robin was transferred from the gun unit to the division's theatrical unit to play violin in a revue called "You Know Me, Al!" Before entertaining the troops in Europe, they performed in New York City. Robert bought box seats and took Katharine to see it. The men were funny parading as

Katharine, 1917.

girls, but otherwise the show was not much, he sourly observed. What it meant from Robin's point of view was he probably would escape being sent to the front lines in France.

Katharine stuck to her nursing course. She also found time to solicit funds for Free Milk for France and to pack cigarettes at an east side tobacco warehouse for soldiers going overseas. She seldom ventured to Wilderstein, although her father, hoping to take advantage of the rare opportunity to see her without distraction from her mother and aunts, sent her many plaintive messages to come. When his gout was not too painful he took long walks with Grace Montgomery, who in the evenings played the ukulele to amuse him. On March 18, Robert carefully wrote in his daybook. "52 weeks ago HMS struck by shell at Zemlak, Albania.; 3/20 died of shock, grave #34 at Koritza." He was deeply touched when a street in Koritza was named after him. It may have been at this time that Robert indexed all his carefully saved daybooks for references to his second-born son.

At the end of the month, with the knowledge and, in fact, the vigorous urging of Daisy and Katharine, Robert entertained at Wilderstein a young woman with whom he had flirted on his last transatlantic crossing. She had been in Daisy's class at Bryn Mawr. Visiting her sister in New York while her husband was in Texas, she had joined the same nursing course as Katharine and quickly let Katharine know she was eager to see her father. Katharine delighted in acting both as catalyst and chaperone. Robert behaved like a star-struck teenager. "Harry says Aunt Nettie must have learnt about H. as the whole family is excited and stirred up," he reported to her. Bessie also wrote Katharine, disdaining to recognize the erotic side of the relationship. "Helvetia certainly seems to have made a great impression on your father and, from all you say, must be decidedly attractive. He always respected and liked people who were serious and he must be glad you have such a capable friend and that you are to work with her." When Bessie returned from the South, Helvetia vanished.

In June, Lieutenant Hambley started weekending nearby in order to court Betty. In late August, he wrote Robert a formal letter declaring his worthiness and love. Robert interviewed him in the library in Betty's presence. Expressing strong sentiments against war marriages, he sought official assurance that Hambley would not be sent overseas for twelve months. That assurance was not forthcoming. Nevertheless, Robert consented to a September 9 wedding and gave Betty a thousand dollars to buy a "new clothes outfit." The ceremony took place late in the afternoon at the Church of the Messiah, in Rhinebeck. The church was packed. Fifty friends and relatives were invited to the reception at Wilderstein.

It may have been as a present to animal-loving Daisy that Robert bought a Norwegian pony and two baby goats shortly afterwards, for he had grounds to believe that she would be the next to leave the family circle. His daybook notes she was "entertaining or acting as guide for a Capt. Lienhan." The captain was actually Charles Lennihan, a man to whom Daisy had been strongly attracted for some time. She had lunched with him alone in Washington when they were changing trains on the way to Spartanburg. (She had joked to Katharine that mama was terrified she was going to elope.) Given a five-day leave from his camp in Maryland, he visited her in North Carolina. Unfortunately, the five days shrunk to a weekend when he received orders to proceed immediately to a camp in Virginia. Daisy had high hopes they would meet again in Washington on her way home, but Bessie could not fix a definite date and, in the end, their schedules did not mesh. Daisy and Charles would stay in contact for years. He made her god-mother to his son and even contemplated buying The Homestead. That they never married may have been a matter of Fate's capricious timing.

That fall Bessie took a political action that must have astonished everyone she knew. She voted in the gubernatorial election. New York State had finally enfranchised its women and, probably urged by Margaret Aldrich, an ardent suffragist, she registered and voted.

During this vibrant period, both Robin and Arthur were in Paris. Robin's violin had settled his fate, but Arthur was still subject to the draft, for the satisfactory life he was leading had resulted in his putting on considerable weight. (He confessed to having acquired a weakness for pastries.) He was now working for the Red Cross in their tuberculosis unit and had been promoted to second lieutenant, with a DeDion automobile and chauffeur at his disposal. Robert's hope for an exemption was based on Arthur's weak eyes. Arthur would not need it. At eleven o'clock on the morning of November 11, 1918, the Armistice was declared. "Huge crowds gathered along the Avenue de l'Opera and the Boulevards, but there was no manifestation until that moment," Arthur wrote his father from the Cercle Artistique et Litteraires, a club he had recently joined. "An hour later all the houses were bedecked with the allied flags, of which the French and American were the

Betty's marriage to Lieutenant Littleton C.F. Hambley, September 9, 1918. Gilbert Hambley, Daisy, Littleton Hambley, Betty, Katharine line up in front of the porte cochere. (The bride's satin wedding dress, tulle veil and satin slippers have been preserved in the Wilderstein collections.)

most conspicuous, while crowds of the different associations walked by singing the Marseillaise and other national songs... It will be very interesting walking in the streets later as the blue-covered lights are being restored to their peace-time brilliancy, an extraordinary contrast after feeling one's way around as we have had to do for the last few years."

Paris quickly recovered its glitter. Arthur stayed on, working for the Red Cross, now at a first lieutenant's pay. In June he attended League of Red Cross meetings in Geneva and during the fall he established a Serbian Hospital in France. For this last achievement, he received a handsome decoration from the Serbian government. In May 1919, he was appointed an inspector in the Red Cross with the "assimilated" rank of captain.

Robin remained in France until February when he was discharged from the army. Eventually he got an office job with the New York City police force. Its main value to him seems to have been that it served as a means of making valuable connections, or at least that is what he told his father. He prided himself on having met the mayor and commissioners at various functions. His pay was only $125 a month, while it cost at least $5,000 a year "to keep up his position," he explained, but at least it paid his city rent.

Daisy made use of her nursing skills at Ellis Island, which had been turned into a receiving station for repatriated soldiers. Every morning, before the sun was up, she took a trolley to the Battery to board the ferry to the island. When the hospital was converted to a facility solely for infectious diseases, she was no longer needed. She soon found another job—right in the family. Betty, living in Salisbury, North Carolina, needed someone to be with her during her last month of pregnancy. Daisy went to her in late May. The baby was born at the end of June, a fine rosy son, named Robert after his proud grandfather. To get him off to the right start in life, he was baptized in the white and gold salon at Wilderstein in the early summer. Daisy would always adore and care for that boy

Daisy, right, with unidentified co-worker, while serving as a nurse's aid in the Red Cross hospital established to receive repatriated servicemen, April 1, 1919. (Daisy's uniform is in the Wilderstein collections.)

in every way she was able. He enlivened all her nurturing instincts.

Katharine had begun the year nursing wounded soldiers in New York's Great Metropolitan Hospital, but that job, too, dried up. With the exception of a visit to Bar Harbor, she spent most of the summer at Wilderstein, playing tennis and golf with Robin and Daisy. In October, it was Daisy's turn to leave the place. She paid her second visit to her Bryn Mawr classmate Mary Lee Hickman in Louisville, Kentucky.

Pleased as he was to have his family close at hand, Robert did not know what to do with himself. His occasional visits to the city were lonely affairs. Often he dined and lunched alone. To while away the time, he read magazines on electricity at the New York Public Library. In the fall he exchanged his Ford touring car and $400 for a wire-wheeled Overland. He sold the *Ellide* and bought a launch that was so long Arthur was afraid it would not fit in the boathouse. All the while, he worried about his deteriorating finances. Many of his stocks failed to pay dividends, his 80th Street house needed a new roof. He nervously recorded his weight at the top of each daybook page—at one point, it was down to 163 13/16. Beneath it he stated whether Slide Mountain in the Catskills was visible, half in or out, veiled in mist and clouds. It seems to have been his way of forecasting the weather.

As usual, Bessie, rented a city apartment for the winter months, this time sharing expenses with her sisters. Robert must have objected to the cost, for she sharply reminded him that he had once freely assumed responsibility for her well-being, that she hardly ever indulged in a theater ticket or any amusement whatever and that she had not bought a winter suit in six years.

As soon as Bessie left Wilderstein for New York, Robert took Katharine and Grace to Switzerland, to spend the winter months of 1920 at Chateau d'Oex. The family "gang" was on the pier to wave them off. Arthur took them to all his favorite haunts in Paris—cocktails at Maxim's, tea and scones in the British Tea Room, a watercolor exhibition at the Cercle Artistique et Litteraires. Robert's reaction was that Arthur looked very fine in a high hat. From Paris Robert and the girls went directly to the Rosat, where the girls occupied the big room that had so often been his. The pension was the social center of Chateau d'Oex that year, with dances, musicale teas, and skating parties galore. Much to Robert's disappointment, Katharine and Grace skied only once and never got on a luge. But they thought nothing of walking the eight miles to Montbovan or Gstaad and back again, a total distance of sixteen miles in each case. Unhappily, Robert was not able to enjoy either the sport or the glorious weather. The train from LeHavre to Paris had been without heat and the chill he got developed into a violent inflammation of his heart and lungs that he simply could not shake. His sleep was broken, he had no appetite; he not only could not ski, skate, or luge, he hardly dared go outside.

In early March he started home, leaving Katharine and Grace at the Hotel de France et Choiseul under the chaperonage of Ninon Newton, whose sole credential was that she was now married. Arthur, who had been offered a post in Russia, turned it down, although he was convinced the Bolshevik revolution was an ephemeral affair. Instead, he accompanied the girls to sunny Florence. They had a wonderful time.

Back at Wilderstein, Robert did a great deal of timed walking. He made it to Wilderstein from Rhinebeck in forty-eight minutes, by way of the Mortons' fields. His pace, as good or better than he had achieved several years previously, served to reassure him that he had not aged or been ill at all. In a state of high euphoria he sent Newman to Buffalo for a Studebaker automobile. Arthur, who was home for a visit, and Katharine were at Wilderstein for most of the summer. Daisy went briefly to Saratoga and then, with Peg, to Yarmouth, Maine, but generally he was surrounded by his family. It may have been for a respite that he and Harry took a steamboat trip to Newfoundland, Canada. In the autumn, while Daisy was making grape juice, he supervised the baling of the hay.

At the end of October, the family began breaking up again. First Arthur returned to Paris; then, just before Christmas, Katharine joined Grace and assorted Montgomerys for another tour of Europe. Once again, the home-rooted "gang" were there to see them off.

Wilderstein ladies gossiping on the verandah. (Left to right) Addie, Betty, Bessie, Nettie, and Daisy.

Robert en route to Newfoundland, late summer 1920. Later Daisy wrote on the reverse: "My father took this trip with my uncle, H. E. Montgomery. As I recall it was the last time he spent a night away from home."

Still, the holiday season in the Hudson Valley was full of the usual social activity. On New Year's Day 1921, Daisy penned a merry letter to Katharine describing the events that filled her calendar. The previous evening, she and Bessie had gone to the Rogers' ball. The Dows were there with a house party of twelve. Vincent Astor and some other men raced all over the dance floor in and on various grandchildren's baby carriages, bicycles, miniature automobiles, and scooters. Monday night was the opera, Tuesday and Wednesday nights dinner with friends. One afternoon, a boy they had known in Spartanburg brought his mother to meet Elizabeth Lynch. The following week she had still another dinner. She wondered how she would survive such a plethora of engagements.

Daisy need not have worried. She did not go to one of them. On January 3, 1921, at seven o'clock in the evening, her father died.

Like his father's, Robert's death was sudden and painless. Having spent New Year's Day in bed feeling poorly, he agreed to be examined by a Kingston specialist. The diagnosis was that his heart was failing and that there was only the slightest chance he would recover. Dropsy set in. He lost consciousness and, like a tired child drifting off to sleep, he died.

Bessie was devastated. "Your father has so filled my mind and life for so many years that it seems as if the bottom were out of everything," she wrote Katharine. "Such an empty void is left. Can you imagine what this house is without him?" No one could.

EPILOGUE

WHEN THEIR FATHER DIED, Robin was thirty-two years old, Arthur thirty, Daisy twenty-nine and the twins twenty-seven. Each responded to his death in distinct, but predictable ways. Arthur and Katharine, who had increasingly distanced themselves from the family, made Europe their home. Arthur migrated from Paris to Monaco as his principal residence. There he built a villa in the form of a tower high above the town on the Nouvelle Corniche. He prudently made it into two apartments, one that he kept for his own use and one that he rented for income. "If you once have an establishment of you own," he wrote Daisy in the early 1930's, "you will never wish to live with others." On the scattered occasions he returned to America, he preferred New York City to Rhinebeck. He stayed in small hotels in Greenwich Village or at the Harvard Club and sought out the best inexpensive bistros in town. When later in life he spent more time at Wilderstein, he took over the white and gold room, piling his personal correspondence and business papers on the onyx-topped tables. Mornings he drove the current Packard to Schermerhorn's where he read his newspapers and drank coffee. Afternoons he played tennis at the Edgewood Club of Tivoli or conversed over tea with his neighbors. Arthur always remained a bit of a boulevardier.

Katharine floated about Europe, where, she told Daisy, "people don't take things so seriously." Then she settled in Paris. For a long time the focus of her life was a romance with a married man who, contrary to her expectations, never intended to divorce his wife. Just before the outbreak of the Second World War, she returned to America and lived in a series of walkups on the fringes of Greenwich Village. Hard pressed for money, she took positions as companion to wealthy women friends traveling to Florida and California. Her tale of a two-week trip from Santa Barbara to the East Coast, alone in an ailing Ford and at a cost of eighty-nine cents a day, is a marvel of independence and resourcefulness. In her last years she returned to Rhinebeck. She did not live at Wilderstein, however, but in a converted schoolhouse east of the village. Much to the distress of the family she shared it with a married couple and seldom came home.

It was Daisy who held the fort at Wilderstein. Little by little she took her father's place as the guiding force of the household. It was not an easy task. Bessie and Robin lived there, too. Both required constant discrete managing. Bessie hovered over Robin, indulging his self-appointed role as sole family decision maker. Progressively more dictatorial, he speculated with jointly held securities, capriciously lavished money on rental properties, and bought mechanical equipment as whim dictated. Arthur commiserated with Daisy and offered advice: "Why don't you try and bring all your problems with Robin down to dollars & cents & talk 1½ hours every month on the subject. Then if this doesn't work ask for a reorganization." He contributed to the upkeep of the establishment, but steered clear of it. In fact, he urged the family to sell all their real property including Wilderstein and Wildercliff.

Daisy's lot became infinitely more trying when Betty, whose family was soon increased by two daughters, gave her inheritance to Littleton who lost it by stubbornly investing in declining cotton stocks. Yet, he refused to seek a paying job. In the early 1930's, the Hambley's came to live at Wilderstein, converting the third floor into a quasi-apartment. Daisy, with some help from Katharine and Arthur, supported them. "Betty is Valsparing in the back hall," she wrote Katharine describing household activities. "We got Newman to mow the lawn yesterday after much talking. Mattison plowed the plot for the vegetable garden, also put the greenhouse in order, all the refuse of the last 40 years being cleaned out so that we may have some vegetables in late April... I think the future of this place will be to get rid of the animals and have tenants in every house, and have just one man to do the garbage, ice and grounds and repairs." As money problems multiplied, she was forced to accept a position as secretary and companion to her Aunt Sophie Langdon. (Never lacking in humor, in private Daisy called her "The Deaconess.") Obliged to spend the winters in New York City and the summers at Mansakenning, she was rarely at Wilderstein.

Then, suddenly, everything changed. Daisy became the friend, indeed, the "closest companion," of Franklin Delano Roosevelt. Fate may have had a hand in it, but that the relationship flourished was due to the strengths and resilience she had developed in the course of her forty years of difficult family life. It was as if everything she was and everything she had done was preparation for it.

Daisy and Franklin had much in common. Both were plucky and graceful survivors. Although Franklin was far more flamboyant, they were both skilled at role-playing. Both were saved from despair not only by faith but by their sense of comedy. Most important, they shared a deep respect for their heritage and a passion for the land that was its foundation. Neither felt whole when living elsewhere than their beloved ancestral homes. In one of her most eloquent outpourings, Daisy wrote Franklin of her situation at

Daisy enjoying a family excursion with President Franklin Delano Roosevelt aboard his yacht, which Daisy had named the *Potomac*, September 8, 1937. Daisy is wearing the beautiful Panama hat he brought to her from Central America.

Aunt Sophie's: "It is strange to be living in someone else's house... The wind in the trees, even, is a strange wind, whereas there is an intimacy with the wind that sighs through the branches of the pines outside my tower window at home—the creakings in the floor, the way the sun slants through the windows—no matter how often you've heard them, they are always strangers compared to the creakings and sunlight at Home—Everything is strange, and perhaps for that reason interesting, in this little world." From time to time Franklin came to tea at Wilderstein. Daisy's diary tells how the family scurried to find enough chairs without broken bottoms so that everyone could sit. Another entry describes settling Franklin on a couch facing the only view of the river that had not become overgrown. But she never complained about the deterioration of her cherished home.

When Sophie Langdon died in August 1941, Franklin arranged for Daisy to work on the Roosevelt family papers destined for the presidential library in Hyde Park, a job she would keep for over twenty years. She became an intimate at the White House and, with a small group of very close friends, provided relaxation for Franklin on his long cross country train trips inspecting munitions factories and selling war bonds. She went to Warm Springs, Georgia, with him. And always she tended Fala, the Scottish terrier she had given him as a puppy in 1940 and who was so often by Franklin's side that to the public he became a symbol for the president. Their companionship was so profound that Franklin even let Daisy fuss about his health. In his last days, he was grateful, even though he joked about it, to receive dietary supplements of gruel from her steady hand. Daisy was with him at Warm Springs when he died in April 1945.

Shortly afterward, she wrote in her diary, "I never felt any self-consciousness or embarrassment, or inhibitions when with him. I could say or think what I wanted... He answered, or did not answer, my questions... He knew that I knew there were many things he could not answer." In his own way Franklin spoke of their relationship from the grave. He had saved her letters. His daughter Anna found them in the stamp box he carried with him wherever he went. Daisy adroitly recovered them and kept them hidden with his letters to her and her diary covering the years 1933 to 1945. Shortly after her death, they were found in her tower bedroom. Roosevelt biographer, Geoffrey C. Ward, edited them. While presenting a unique view of both their personalities, his book *Closest Companion* (Houghton Mifflin, 1995) offers firsthand glimpses of Wilderstein during those years.

On Christmas Day 1953, Bessie suddenly and peacefully died. "She was one of the survivors of the Victorians, now none too many," a friend from Sunday school days wrote, summing up her life. Her death left a void, but it also gave her children new freedom. They sold Wildercliff and the Gate Lodge. Betty, now widowed, was given the Wildercliff farm house, refurbished and named Villa Saga. Katharine died in 1970, Robin in 1974 and Arthur in 1975. None suffered long illnesses.

Wilderstein and its outbuildings continued their steady decline and, in 1983, Daisy placed them in the care of Wilderstein Preservation. Even then she reserved life occupancy. Every afternoon at four o'clock she served tea to Betty, who would live to be ninety-three, and to whomever dropped in. She also mowed stretches of lawn and fetched pans and buckets when water ran through breaks in the roof. She drove to town for shopping and lunch. Well into her nineties, she relished a spin in an antique iceboat on the frozen Hudson River.

In 1989, a young local carpenter was hired to repair the decayed sashes of Wilderstein's tower windows. He and Daisy became friends. One afternoon she climbed the steep stairs to the top floor to see how the work was progressing. "This is my favorite place in the whole house," she told him. "When I was a little girl I asked my mother where I came from. She answered that I came in through a top tower window on a sunbeam. One of these days I shall go out on a moonbeam."

On June 29, 1991, in her hundredth year, Margaret Lynch Suckley died quietly at Wilderstein. Perhaps, her great spirit did waft away on a moonbeam. Still some trace remains. Of all the handsome houses on the banks of the Hudson River, Wilderstein preserves most vibrantly the sense of the family who built it and made it their home.

ACKNOWLEDGEMENTS

Wilderstein and the Suckleys: A Hudson River Legacy is based on the extraordinarily wide variety of materials in the Wilderstein Preservation collections. Spanning over two hundred continuous years and containing the Suckleys' own toys, tools, sports equipment, and clothing as well as correspondence, books, and photographs, they provide an unparalleled resource for interpreting the house, its outbuildings and its landscaped grounds. The manuscript collection alone measures over seven hundred linear feet of documents that include such items as sheet music, electric appliance advertisements, school report cards, and theater tickets in addition to letters, journals, bills, and checkbooks. The eclectic, highly personal book collection numbers approximately seven thousand volumes.

Wilderstein's photographic collection, beginning in the 1840's, is remarkable both for its breadth and its quality. The images range from snapshots taken by family members with early hand-held cameras to portraits by prestigious studio photographers. There are at least twenty thousand of them. Each enhances and vivifies the written record. All quotations and photographs, unless noted, are from the Wilderstein archives.

All along the way, the making of this book has been a collaborative process. Every Suckley who created and saved family papers, photographs and books had a hand in it; we salute them posthumously. More immediate were the generous contributions of colleagues. The gratitude I and future researchers owe to Duane Watson, President of Wilderstein Preservation, and to Linda Watson, archivists par excellence, for making the collections accessible is incalculable. George B. Davis, who is inventorying the books, both as a grantee of the New York State Conservation/Preservation Program and as a volunteer, has offered countless insights only his sources could provide.

From the outset, it was clear that the vitality of the Suckleys' story would spring from the interplay of text and image. Anne Liljedahl Schock, Conservation Fellow, began managing the care of the photographic material over a year ago under a grant from the Kress Foundation and continues her work with a New York State Conservation/Preservation Program grant. It was my good fortune to have her as an ongoing guide in choosing the photographs and in identifying elusive subjects, dates and photographers.

The facts and comments offered by countless friends were a constant encouragement. John Winthrop Aldrich, Deputy Commissioner of the New York State Office of Parks, Recreation and Historic Preservation and one of the founders of Wilderstein Preservation, first introduced me to the archives and, from his vast fund of historical knowledge, has prevented inadvertent errors from creeping into the text. For those that remain, I take full responsibility and invite correction.

My research for this book was initially funded by the New York State Council on the Arts. An article on the period from 1852 to 1897 resulting from that grant was published in *The Hudson Valley Regional Review*, Vol. 7, No. 2. My work on *Wilderstein and the Suckleys: A Hudson River Legacy* was funded by a grant from Furthermore, the publication program of the J. M. Kaplan Fund.

CYNTHIA OWEN PHILIP